BLUE DUSK

By Madeline DeFrees

POETRY

Double Dutch (chapbook), 1999
Possible Sibyls, 1991
Imaginary Ancestors, 1991
The Light Station on Tillamook Rock, 1990
Magpie on the Gallows, 1982
When Sky Lets Go, 1978
From the Darkroom, 1964

PROSE

Later Thoughts from the Springs of Silence, 1962
Springs of Silence, 1953

BLUE DUSK

Madeline DeFrees

New & Selected Poems, 1951–2001

 COPPER CANYON PRESS

Cover art: Morris Graves (1910–2001) *Winter Bouquet # 17*, 1973. Watercolor and tempura on paper. Museum of Northwest Art, Collection of Marshall and Helen Hatch. Photograph by T. Kelly.

Copper Canyon Press is in residence under the auspices of the Centrum Foundation at Fort Worden State Park in Port Townsend, Washington. Centrum sponsors artist residencies, education workshops for Washington State students and teachers, blues, jazz and fiddle tunes festivals, classical music performances, and The Port Townsend Writers' Conference.

LIBRARY OF CONGRESS CATALOGING-IN-PUBLICATION DATA

DeFrees, Madeline.

Blue dusk: new and selected poems, 1951–2001

/ Madeline DeFrees. — 1st ed.

p. cm.

ISBN 1-55659-166-7 (alk. paper)

1. Women — Poetry.   I. Title.

PS3554.E4 B58 2001

811'.54 — DC21

2001003559

3 5 7 9 8 6 4 2

FIRST PRINTING

COPPER CANYON PRESS

Post Office Box 271

Port Townsend, Washington 98368

www.coppercanyonpress.org

For all my students over the years,
whose creativity and commitment to writing
have nourished my own work.

Nothing exists without its complement:
the orange dawn advances toward blue dusk...

Contents

New Poems

2001

from *From the Darkroom*
1964

from *When Sky Lets Go*
1978

from *Magpie on the Gallows*
1982

from *The Light Station on Tillamook Rock*
1990

from *Imaginary Ancestors*
1991

from *Possible Sibyls*
1991

BLUE DUSK

New Poems

Going Back to the Convent

This time it is no dream. After twenty-three years away
I wake in a Spokane convent in my Black Watch
plaid pajamas — daybreak, the last
day of September 1996. I used to spring from bed
at the bell's first clang. Now there's
something wrong with the bedsprings
I cannot fix.

      Shyly, light enters, spills over
the floor of the room. Holy or not, I
feel more at home than in thirty-eight
years I lived here. Then let me admit the light,
endorse the mirror over my private
sink. Time to reopen the old account
stored in the memory bank.

      What was I running from
or into? The uneasy light of the senior
prom? Mother's dream of a child bride, supported by
pennies from heaven? Or was it the writing
life laid as a sacrifice to a jealous god
on the tomb of the woman
I'd hoped to become?

      Whatever it was, it will soon
be over. I write this now to reclaim it.

Shackleton

... the deep contentments of desolation

ANTHONY LANE

Two faces of the same coin: poet and explorer. This
is Shackleton's third
expedition to the Antarctic since he had a vision
of the ice — still more, of isolation.
He calls the ship *Endurance* after a family motto
By Endurance We Conquer. The boat is made of
Norwegian fir and planks of oak
sheathed in greenheart. Wood so sturdy
it cannot be worked by ordinary means.

Adventure draws a poet's crew: men of imagination
able to claim, transform, and name
whatever comes to hand: seals   spars   penguins
blubber   ice.   The mercies of their universe are few —
sleep without watch that merges into death, dangers
they cannot know before they are delivered.
Mirage engulfs them: frost-smoke
curled skyward like a prairie fire, land
on the near horizon.

                    The pressure of the ship against
pack ice duplicates the pressure of a poem
looking for escape through a crack in the skull.
The writer steers his craft toward open water, hoping
for a lead in the frozen sea. He finds a way through
the complex syntax of drift and floe
and the rococo architecture of the hummocks. Follows

the maze of memory to a downpour
of sudden light.

               By night the ship's photographer
drives into the face of the moon. He sets a flash
behind each chunk of ice that
moors *Endurance*. Ice flowers should have telegraphed
a warning. They spread pale pink on water
like a carpet of carnations. Carnations are a
boutonniere in Death's lapel but serve as well for
weddings. For now Shackleton's boat rides at anchor
destined to go down, a bride of the sea.

On Western Avenue behind a Horse-and-Buggy

We drive at a slow trot behind the Clydesdale's
white fetlocks. You ask, *Is that horse*
wearing spats? It's a joke, but I can tell, from
the voltage of your attention, a poem
is on the way. What you are seeing, I can only
guess. I'm back in seventh-grade

                         Agriculture
class. No rich farm dirt under my fingernails.
Already I know by heart everything
the textbook can teach me. Eager to recite, head
seeded with facts for the state exam,
I am on my own. Nothing and

                    no one can touch me.
But my classmates remember the studhorse
mounting the brood mare. They were with her when
she dropped her foal. And the words
from the book — too stiff and starched like my dress —
almost antiseptic,

                will never fool them. Under
cover of the desk, boys deliver
rude gestures. They titter and point. I try to be
nonchalant, keep my grip on the reins,
feet in the stirrups,
star in the onlooker's role.

Through a Silver Screen

A well of light rises from the theater organ pit
where Arnold rehearses the very same pieces
he will play this afternoon
when we come back for the Saturday matinée.
Everywhere else is pitch-black except the red
EXITs. I am alone in this huge space
with the cousin I adore: starstruck watching
the glow pick up the white, open-necked shirt of
my hero, follow the curve of his throat upward
and, like a misplaced halo,
drown in his dark hair.

                    He's eleven years older,
cousin not really my cousin, son of my mother's
adoptive brother. A fact my neighbor points out:
You might grow up and marry Arnold.
Right now, I focus on his hands, fingers assured
as those of José Feliciano, blind from birth.
My fingers turn up at the ends. Piano hands,
Arnold says, proposing we trade. When a man
asks a woman for her hand, doesn't that mean
something? What we have in common: the King's
English, the French words Arnold taught me.

At home, orchestra members will gather to play
their newest toy — flute, trumpet, or
clarinet — on Arnold's arrangements. In her easy-
chair beauty parlor, my little sister will climb
onto the drummer's lap to comb
his thick brown curls. And for the seventeenth

time, Arnold will go over the correct
fingering for the song I'm determined to learn.
He'll wait out my awkward
try: "If you were the only girl in the world
and I were the only boy."

Clematis montana

Flocks of itinerant stars, flung from night's
dome, alight on the caged
expanse of my chain-link fence. I thank them for
partial release from my winter prison.
Constellations of small, pale
birds — grace notes on a steel clef — read a
perennial score, riff of a new season.

When I pause for the seventh time by the south
window, cascades of cabbage butterflies
arrange themselves in bridal
bouquets, fly off with my cabbage heart. Later,
their scent will grow sweeter, their
honey-vanilla fragrance freight the air.
Watching them

              shiver and hover brings back
Ann Lovejoy's glimmer of undiluted joy
as I hear white water
churn over the hard falls into the holding
pool of the soul's wide summer.

Visiting Sunday: Convent Novitiate

The parlor doors shall be glazed, the Custom Book
says, *to facilitate supervision.* Each time
the doorbell rings, the Sister Portress
glides over the gleaming hardwood of the foyer
to greet the families come for their allotted
forty-five minutes a month. Ever the Guardian Angel,
she seats the guests,

                    goes back to wait for others.
From the practice room off the parlor,
Cole Porter's "Night and Day"
seeps under the door, flows over the transom
as my cousin Arnold begins to play
my favorite song: the forbidden worldly music.
Orchestra member, composer,

                        arranger, this is
the cousin who knows how to transpose on sight.
And now the shadow of the portress
crosses the frosted glass. Quickly, Arnold coaxes
the upright piano into a classic
stance, modulates smoothly into the Paderewski
Minuet in G.

               What a moment of triumph for me!
My versatile cousin, the artist
holding the bloodhounds at bay. The portress,
no doubt, reproaches herself for alarm of the ear:
she must have misheard. No miscreants here.

Just dear devotees of traditional music. She taps
twice with her ring, pops open the door,

waits to be introduced. Arnold flashes his heart-
melting smile. I mention his "Mass of the Bells."
Premiered, I add, at St. Joseph Church
in Capitola, California. The portress asks God
to bless us, moves on.
Arnold slips me his latest love song, asks me
to write the lyric.

Almanac

Into my ravaged garden as into the tattered
cocoon of the season
I walk in mud-caked shoes, stalking the last
anorexic string-bean,
the bolting bitter lettuce,
tomatoes defiantly green on the vine,
and bony zucchini.

               None of us wants to go back
to the worm-riddled earth we sprang from.
Already a lachrymose wind
grieves over the ground of our being. And who,
when scarlet letters
flutter in air from sumac and maple,
will be there to

              receive them? Only a sigh
on the wind in the land of bending willow
attending the frost and snow
as they spread a weedy cover. Or a furrow's trace
on the fallow bed where rain
describes a river: the waters of oblivion
I follow crossing over.

Elegy for Arnold

Proclaim Liberty throughout all the land unto all
the inhabitants thereof.

LEVITICUS 25:10 — INSCRIPTION ON THE
LIBERTY BELL

Alone in my living room, I let waves of the music
wash over me: Debussy's "Submerged Cathedral,"
a legendary structure rising
at daybreak from the drowned city. Plainsong joined
to the pagan rite of the sea. The marriage
reminds me of you, Arnold, my not-quite cousin,
and your "Mass of the Bells" forever lost to me.

Three years after I returned to the world, you
left it on Bicentennial Day.
Of this, I remember nothing. How could you
slip away and I not know? As if you were merely
a blip on the heart monitor? If my heart
were hollow as a bell, it would crack for the second
time as Liberty cracked when it tolled

John Marshall's burial, fifty-nine years after being recast.
An armchair traveler headed east,
I visit the bell — flawed still — in Philadelphia's
Independence Hall. Cast early as The Rich Young Nun,
I surrendered my name, shook the dust
of home from my feet, chose the only way
that seemed safe: motif of a fantasy life adrift

on mystical seas. *Dead to the world*, I declared
myself, though my breath might still
cloud a mirror held to the mouth, had I taken
the trouble to consult one. In the rush to
dependence, a mirror crashed from its frame as I
clung to the promised hundredfold. Sometimes
in my dream theater, I hear the gutted chords of

Debussy's prelude, tranquil waves, and eventual
roar of the tide. If you were not
here beside me in the diving bell, I would surely
drown. But I know you've come back
to guide me, reading the difficult score, breathing
the rarefied, music-drenched air
of a love come into its own.

The Paradise Tree

Framed in my window, this birch in winter drab —
long strands blown horizontal in the gale —
reminds me of a woman caught in dishabille,
weeping, of course, and clutching at her robe.
She owes her body to her sleeping husband's rib,
without him, would be incomplete, and still
her gaze strays outward past the farthest hill,
the stranger's word, she thinks, a shade too glib.

Knowing how soon the picture-perfect stales,
she's heard that virtue is its own reward,
a paltry one that turns the spirit slack.
Enclosure is the ambience of jails
and love's the angel with the flaming sword
who guards the gate, prevents her going back.

Surgery Waiting

Supine on a gurney below the Acropolis tacked
to the ceiling, my right leg slowly turning
cement, I'm an accidental artifact of Pompeii
preserved in the cast of history. This is
the way I solidify my position, fully awake
except for the limb no longer connected
to my brain, chatting with the anesthesiologist.

Here in the shadow of the Parthenon, hair veiled
from view like a medieval nun, what I really need
is a hard hat for this major foot reconstruction.
Pale curtains drawn around me for the epidural
or the nerve block. They are like the virginal
curtains of the novices' dormitory
fifty-eight years ago. Now it's IV time

and a member of the team, with a single thrust,
boldly enters my bloodstream. I am wheeled out
feetfirst, to the operating theater, delivered up
to scalpel and saw. Before the cock crows
three times, I will be struck as foretold
from the ground I stand on, my log of a leg lifted
for the thigh-high tourniquet. *What you have to do*

do quickly. Betrayer and betrayed, I carry the Parthenon
with me, its colonnade of perfect form, record of
shifting attachments: Athens, Santa Sophia, the Virgin
Mary, and the Turkish mosque. Twelve of us gathered
in the narrow chamber: I feel the cut, remember to ask,
Is it I, Lord? Is it I? already swayed by the outcome,
the processional frieze over the Judas foot.

Still Life

> The question that he frames in all but words
> Is what to make of a diminished thing.
>
> ROBERT FROST, "THE OVEN BIRD"

After your letter arrived I left the oven on
all night and never once
put my head in it. After your letter arrived
I let one foot follow the other
through the better part of the day. Your letter
lay on the kitchen table by the paring
knife on the stoneware plate with the apple core
like a Dutch still life restored to
its muted color.

              In the sink a spiral of lemon
peel twisted like smoke toward the past and I
think that I let it lie.
The first day of night these eyes you opened
were glassed and dry as your late martini.
The next they brimmed into morning.
It was time to rehearse the Sunday phone call,
the new role laid out for learning.
When you asked,

              Did you get my letter? I picked up
the cue as if you had wired me
roses in winter or proposed
a pas de deux. Then partly for your sake I taught
myself to sing the best song I could make:
the burden of the oven bird's diminished thing. Sang

wash of sunlight on the sill and apple core,
sang water glass half full of emptiness. Sang body
all in shadow that I must bathe and dress.

Balancing Acts

At 47, Hope's driven to find her feet in construction.
She crawls the hip roof of her house like a cat burglar,
gives herself plenty of rope, lashed to
the chimney. In her left hand, she carries a loaded
staple gun. Her right grips the insubstantial.

Cordless phone in my lap, I watch at 74, from my rented
wheelchair, fingers tattooing 9-1-1.
Let me hop with the help of the Sunrise Medical Guardian
to the open door to rehearse
our common fate. We are Siamese joined by a bungee

cord at the inner ear, that delicate point of balance.
Every day we devise new methods
of locomotion. When my walker, upset by a comforter,
collapses to the floor and takes me
with it, I want to reverse the digits:

four and seven, seven and four. Yesterday, Hope wrestled
the circular saw over the edge
where she clung to the ridge and tripped on the safety
cord. It was then I heard the Sirens
wooing Ulysses tied to the mast. Twilight hangs fire

in the west, then snuffs it out. Behind the slant roof
of a dormer, Hope disappears. Two ladders
reach into the void. Is that white flash a sneakered
foot in search of a rung? I conjure a cloudy head
between the smokestack and the evergreen.

No matter how I strain, I cannot bring her back.
Reluctantly I fiddle with the blind,
hear a tune old as the burning of Rome as I weave
between the cave and the whirlpool for a saving
equilibrium. What if I call her Faith,
the evidence of things unseen?

Memory Tract

> Women and elephants never forget an injury.
>
> SAKI

If camels were first to carry the weight — a hump
on the back — of injury unforgiven,
the trait, transferred to the elephant, predictably
fell to women. We forget
more than we remember, but there are exceptions.
Pity the poor savant

              who staggers under this burden:
the population of Calcutta, the square root of
too many odd numbers, exact dimensions of the world's
largest oak. Wood from that tree
boasts memory, a universal property of matter.
Given water, pores of the tabletop
relax the old injury,

              resume their former shape.
Should chance bring players together
for a card game around that table, will a moment of
dumb luck obscure the fact
that Chance has no memory? Will the winner risk
everything he owns, succumb
to the Gambler's Fallacy?

              I own that age has
put a dent in the smooth mechanics of retrieval.
The tip-of-the-tongue phenomenon besets
the brains of all but the very young, thanks to cue

overload. All of which brings us back to a heavy
hump, to camel and elephant, to
much-maligned women who never forget an injury.

Metempsychosis

After a week, unbalanced on one foot, I know why
they call the great blue heron
Big Cranky. Some farmers call them cranes, as if
they were mere weight lifters, which
in a sense, they are.

          I watch the big bird from
an evil star, honking across the sky. Every day
I drag my plaster-of-paris leg past the archer
on one knee lying in wait, past hunters
riding full tilt across the Karastan rug to their
hounds. I would have made a great

               heron with my
movable metatarsal, shifting my bulk to the front of
my foot, although my surgeon implies
that I'm not a fully evolved human. He saws through
bone, inserts

        three screws to help it fuse and pins
four toes to point them in a northerly
direction. Why do I think of animal rights and tales
of vivisection? When I fly south in my wheelchair,
appendages neatly folded, at other
times extended,

        my wingspread matches the Great Blue's.
We are, in truth, the upper crust of
heronry, brooding and solitary. Days go by as we

flap toward bodies of water,
our croaks and calls

                          too often unreturned. I am worn
down to a wren, to the hollow
bone and broken flight that will not mend. Beyond
the riverbank, my semicircular canals
refuse to balance. Yet I do my best to sing, my

last year's nest under the wing of nine full choirs
of pagan muses and Christian
angels. Each day I put my trust in transmigration.

Woman Locked in a Memorial Museum

Her lips remain sealed as the walled south face
of museums admitting no outer light.
Her eyes choose privacy glass
to shield their exclusive color. She follows
the blood's anemic brush against a limited
palette: white-primed canvas
betraying one wish — a hush in the winter landscape
and heart to tell it.

               If she were not so locked
away, so abstracted, would she hear the plash of
water in the garden where dim figures
come and go at the margins? Lured to the other
side, the sculptured ear, turned stone,
closes on its only sound: the nightbird
in the courtyard calling.

                  She wants to go down
the withdrawn face of the mountain in the dark
of the moon. Wants to escape the wan
light thrown from a solitary direction. Nothing
detains her here in the souvenir
snare of the past: these white reflections
in a still basin when the fountain
comes finally to rest.

To Marilyn Monroe Whose Favorite Color
Was White

When you wriggled onto the silver screen, Marilyn —
honey blonde or platinum — I was a nun. I
found you too late in your satin sleep. Now, three
decades past, I grieve from that ancient
cloister, the alabaster body, my beautiful buried
sister. Convent movies had to be clean as
bleach. Even your titles

                      went wrong: *All About Eve.*
The Seven Year Itch. The Asphalt Jungle.
Some Like It Hot. How to Marry a Millionaire.
Sex was a bullet I dodged, that shot on the subway
grate! Skirts lifted to seventh
heaven, you scared me all right, as you scared your
jealous husband.

                   Yet Joe was your friend in the end
as I hope to be. Bride at sixteen like you, given
another name, I was cast with the world's invisible
millionaire. We didn't know who we were,
Norma Jean, too young to care. Even now I imagine
you posed — a pinup everywhere woman who did it
for fifty dollars. I resent

                  the photographer smirking
away with the loot: the generous milky
breasts and bottom, pout of a wounded child. Too bad,
the bad life fate guaranteed you:
dashing absent father, unmarried mother who

had to be locked away. Say *cheese*, Marilyn. Open
those pearly gates,

              come back with me to my former
marmoreal splendor: the lily-pad I escaped
that was never my passion. Ivory walls, skulls in
our heads all day. Snowy sheets and colorless
towels. Chaste linens framing the parchment faces.
It was color I missed most of all,
white sister. I hated the pallor. I want you to play

this part over. I want to barge in as your crazy
mother stealing the scene: capsules
washed down the drain in a lethal river. The beauty
startled awake in the last act from that
white sleep history promised.

Scarecrow Gardens

Late-summer squash put out to sea
in coastal storms. All day, wet
leaves let go. I cut down three
sunflowers, a foot through the heart.
Their dried crowns counsel me to turn
my head and pierce the cloud.
As van Gogh understood, gold comes
in many forms: the best is art.

Peregrine Falcons in the Bank Tower

In wildness is the preservation of the world
THOREAU

Perhaps in cities lies the preservation of the wild
ADRIENNE ROSS

Over the surrogate cliff of a skyscraper, Stewart
courts Virginia: peregrine falcons
named for neighboring streets. His mile-long drives
rival the Blue Angels': figure eights, barrel rolls,
aerial somersaults — all at breath-
taking speed. Soon the whole city of Seattle
is looking up.

              Friends of the Earth will tell you
a rara avis needs no equity.
Landlords build the pair a home — a safe
deposit box for nest-eggs. Through a hole
drilled in the wall, a camera-eye tracks the clutch
as three chicks hatch on the east
ledge of floor fifty-six

                 of the Washington Mutual
Tower. Interest compounds daily, a daily watch
around the lobby monitor. Tragedy
waits in the wings. One afternoon in Freeway Park,
an office-worker eating lunch
later reports a crunching sound, a thud, as a
dead falcon drops

at her feet. Felled by mirrored
skies, Virginia cedes her reveries
to a metropolitan wild. Bankers declare a time of
civic mourning. Shut down the monitor.
Announce a public account for the motherless chicks.
Life on the ledge turns cliff-hanger. Somebody leaves
a yellow rose on the sidewalk.

                        Transferred to
foster-care, chicks grow and thrive. A slightly
older eyas moves in with Stewart
to keep solicitude alive. Another switch
bankrolls a sweet reunion. Fledglings scratch
and flutter as Dad brings home
a fat pigeon, a starling.

                    Even so, two chicks
don't make it. And where is the lone
lost darling whose peregrinations take her into
Fremont? Test-flights explore
the startling reaches where her father courts
another mate. The Emerald City welcomes Bell, who
goes along, accepts the bait,

                       pairs with Stewart
four seasons — and more to come. On every downtown
street, bird-watchers wait for banded
birds' return. These falcons reconstruct Seattle's
skyline. Their crossbow silhouette, a ready-made
reminder of a disappearing breed:
flights of imagination leaving no room for regret.

Widows Riding Amtrak

for Abe Opincar

        hurtle through night tunnels
toward anywhere-but-home, dim lights
of the station ahead, castanet click of the track.
Wherever a listener waits,
the widow tells one story, details fanning out like a
search party. Why would she try to revamp
the comforting bedroom suite, faded La-Z-Boy
under the unlit lamp, except to erase
the living past?

        This journey's preview of the live
show at the next stop begins with
the courtship. One tear for the sterling character
of her husband's devotion
enshrined in a fog of omissions. Then the wedding:
she rises to reenact the walk down the aisle,
lurches a little, clutching the perfect
bouquet to her breast. Strains of *Lohengrin*
in a voice-over version make way for
the bride, taking care not to

        uncouple the bridal
train that stretches into the next car in a dazzle
of satin. Every widow rehearses her own
sad story, openly weeping. Fresh scent of sweet peas
and stephanotis gives way to
funereal wreaths: calla lilies, carnations.

The women feel almost ready for sisters and distant
cousins at the end of the line.
Their enemy is anomie and time that would erode
the last remaining link.

Sapphires in the Mud

> When you buy rubies and sapphires, you own
> the rainbow.
>
> ROLAND NEFTULE, GEM DEALER,
> IN *National Geographic*

If splinters of the True Cross in the Talisman
of Charlemagne are held in place
by fake sapphires
pressed together — one cabochon, a pale
blue glass through the loupe of the trained
gemologist; the other, mere
quartz — how can we trust the authentic

at the heart of this counterfeit world? Standing
on my own front porch, I'm talking to Dave,
my favorite plumber, a man who went
straight from high school into the Coast Guard
and then, I suppose, to his present
unglamorous calling. His hobby is finding and
cutting sapphires, even the half-carat

stones: no jewel too trivial in that alluvium
for the patient hand and eye. "I like looking
almost as well as cutting," Dave says.
Cobalt, canary, and blush, the stones are made of
corundum — hexagonal crystals forged
in rolling magma, tossed in the riverbed, and flushed
to the surface. Repeatedly buried in silt.

Trace metals determine the colors. Precise ratio
of chrome creates rubies, the rarest of all.
But not in Montana where paler gems are the rule.
The seeker of rubies courts danger,
sets himself up for a fall. Consider these shady
Burmese stalking a military jeep
in the streets of Myanmar. They're out to filch

taillights, tumble them in gravel, back them with
foil, and hawk them to tourists.
Ruby crystals for the True Believer! It's never
that easy. Dave on his hands and knees, eyes
panning the ground, scooping it up. He grovels in
mud and dreck, filling the bowl.
Rinses the load, and shakes the tray so the heaviest

gems will settle, flips everything upside down
culling jewels from dross, one genuine stone at a time,
making the rainbow his own, already
dreaming the gold pendant
holding the incredible cross.

Hanging the Blue Nuns

for Warren Carrier

Like saints in cathedral windows, they look
from their looking-glass scene
into the deep blue pool of the viewer
unveiled, whose head hovers
over the evergreens, the lake and frozen field.
I thought of you when I hung them,
two framed Blue Nuns, released from a Portland
bar. They carried me back to the year
you hired me away from

                    the convent. Remember
the day you brought me a gift of
Blue Nun wine? With exquisite tact you taught me
its German name — *Liebfraumilch* — the literal
milk of Our Lady, and parties became
a religious observance. Warren, this morning I'm
flying high over your home state
on my way to a dry Kentucky town to read
my poems. Not one

                    Blue Nun in all of Calloway
County. I'm hoping to raise the ante
by reading my Blue Nun verse. Of course, there's
that other nun, also blue, whose stone
at the back of my brain is a monument to revision.
How do we know the lives that collared us
from those we hoped to star in? Nostalgia swirls
a screen of smoke and mirrors — camouflage for
errors — over the shrine of the past.

Double Dutch

Dutch on both sides of his family tree — now I can
say it — this was my father's history.
The Mennonite blood of his grandparents, a peaceful
tide in his veins, kept my bookkeeper father
a farmer at heart like men
in the ancestral lines.

                Mother adopted the Irish,
knowing less of Vermeer than she knew of her own
flesh and blood. He would have painted her
Dutch, and that was Mother's *bête noire*. A phrase
to please her because it comes from France.
Against the odds, she Frenchified Dad, denied his
inheritance.

                Confused and out of touch, I lived that
double lie, an alien among the Dutch, shadowed
on either side by French illusion, Irish myth.
The legacy I traveled with
extended to the playground. North and south,
eggbeater ropes coming at me. Trapped between, I
swallowed the heart in my mouth — Irish — and bounced
like a Mexican bean.

If I beat the Dutch out of my
classmates, tied everyone in French knots, it was
only a game. In a children's book, I
discovered the Scots renamed Double Dutch
Double French. They were a match for Mother. And
Dad? Forty years underground, he deserves
this retraction: *Dear Dad, I admit,*
the French and Irish were fiction. I'm on your side.
I'm Dutch.

Vermeer's *A Woman Holding a Balance*

Picture-within-a-picture closed on themselves: a
Chinese box of interiors.
And the low-lying path of lemon riverlight
welling over the woman, is she
the source or the mouth?

                          Figures in the frame teem
with meaning: jewel box, mirror, pearl strands,
Last Judgment on the wall. The glow through a high
window shows a blue robe on the table
and — best of all — the balance scale
held in the woman's hand.

                          Together, the symbols
tell a story, oblique and contradictory.
Their import is uncertain, but scholars weigh in
anyway. They say the woman
stands for Vanity. They say that her life is
in balance.

                Critics comb the centuries for icons
to translate. They cite revealed religion,
predestination, Time's triumph
over things of this world. The woman holding
a balance keeps her silence. The artist lies

engraved beyond the vanishing point of the canvas.
Vermeer did not sign this work or name it,
but others supplied the lack: The Goldweigher,

Girl Weighing Pearls, A Woman Holding a Balance.
Whatever it's called

             the painting calls us back to
recompense it gives. Light loves the woman's face,
her dress: see how it lingers.
In suspended light, what's being weighed is too
small for the naked eye, too large
for the pans to contain: detail that prompted one

viewer to consult a microscope and swear that
the scale held nothing. The painting, like all of
Vermeer, is reflexive, embodies a Chinese
patience. It echoes with incertitude. No matter
how we try, we cannot pin it down.

                    The woman
stands pensive and alone. She invites us to enter
the painting. Objects in the foreground
bar the way. Between the artist and the viewer, an
impassable gulf that widens as we
try to cross it. The painting means: itself.

FROM

From the Darkroom

Requiem Mass: Convent Cemetery

The shaft of their Gregorian cuts clean:
through the domed summer, through the bare brightness,
through the long shadows of the sycamore arching
over white crosses where the bones molder
under the leveling loam.

Life shrinks to a pair of names
(born into one, the other worn with the veil)
and a single date, her entrance to eternity:
May eight, February three, March ten, and then
four digits, juggled a bit by time
in the wry manner of a clock's ticking
and a calendar's canceled sheet.

All the fierce drama,
too big for Broadway and Hollywood
to frame in footlights or celluloid,
told without glamour on a wedge of stone,
cut from its context: the common life, inviolably alone,
each in the same alphabet as the next,
save for the abstract language of moss and lichen
on the cold concrete.

Sparrows divide the stillness; we repeat,
Unto Thy faithful... life is changed...
He will not let them fall. Veiled heads bow low,
calling Him out of silence with the priest,
calling Him with the bells to come:
Absolve, Domine.

Changed life, not taken; or taken, kept —
bold word, transcending sunlight and the probing root
that cracks the footstone where our Sisters lie.
Dark hides the ways they traveled by,
these solitary, single hearts, quickened by the same love
in a million guises.

Disguises, rather, for we seldom see
from above the tombstones. Only now and then
between the Introit and the last Amen,
here in the cemetery,
we look and gauge our place and look away.

A Kind of Resurrection

Bruised by the wintry air
the Dead Sea apples hold
rigorously to boughs
from which the weight has rolled,
lean to the lengthening light
here in the tree's shadows.

Fused to the twig's bold spear
locked in each open side,
harvest dissolves in ash
the dwindling season's load
and reconciles in night
the hale, the hectic flush.

Closed on its riddled core,
impermeable to sun,
flesh brandishes the thorn
by which it was undone
and wears the snow-tomb's white
silence with unconcern.

Nuns in the Quarterlies

Used as accents in a landscape or seaview,
upright in merciful black on the sand's monotone —
not even the devil's advocate could question
their purely decorative purpose. Like fountains in Rome
and eagles hanging over cliffs,
they are all suggestion,
posing no problem deeper than the eye.

But if the memory persist in asking why, an evening frolic
through slicker pages of the thicker magazines
where nuns drift in and out of nightmare scenes,
yields complementary answers, all symbolic:
Woman, the ancient lie, the unattainable mystery,
the apple high on paradisal branches,
the history of heaven and hell, of fall and pardon,
innocence unmasked in God's own Garden.

Naive, perhaps, or else inscrutable:
like Mona Lisa or like Whistler's Mother?
The things they do not say are always quotable,
and unknown quantities reduce the other
terms to their just equivalent. Nuns are the fictions
by whom we verify the usual contradictions.

The Outsider

Diagonals of mindless snow
cover my tracks and blur the cloud
of frosty breath on silence hung
the darkening way I walk along.

Scant leaves I cannot shake echo
with voices from the startled wood:
their cries are brittle, sighs are pronged
and night declines them frozen-tongued.

Under the ice lulled currents go
brokenly. Sealed in pools of shade
the fishes lie that leaped among
ripples of light and waves of song.

Antique Convent Parlor

Flowers would only die in the fluted bowl,
sighing for parallel sun through shuttered dark,
there where the chimney lamp's globular shades,
hand-painted with violets
in china four times larger than life,
gather no moths.

Visitors slowly stiffen in high-backed chairs,
restless against the carved and clustered grapes,
prodded by heads of unimaginable fowls
where duck-bills and foliage meet
in a songless aviary.

Even the peacock cushion in needlepoint
covers its softness with indifferent plastic;
and heavy, gold-framed mirrors, swung from chains,
give back the crystal chandelier
above the ornamental hearth.

High on their walnut shelves, locked in from touch,
museum pieces, wrought in glass and gold,
wear names that ring and spiral through the air:
amberine and cranberry glass, Vaseline glass epergne,
German bisque ware, sand majolica;
and prisms, prisms and bangles everywhere.

A nun walks into the fretted and frescoed welter,
impersonal and ageless in linear serge;
pauses beside the alabaster urn
and with a patient hand
outwits the pilfering dust.

Skid Row

Out of the depths have I cried, O Lord,
Where the lean heart preys on the hardened crust,
Where short wicks falter on candle-hopes
And winter whips at a patchwork trust.

From darkened doorways no welcome shines,
No promise waits up the broken stair,
And the coin that summons the night with wine
Buys a morning of sick despair.

Out of the depths have I cried in vain
And the still streets echo my lonely calls;
All the long night in the moaning wind
The bruised reed breaks and the sparrow falls.

Long Day's Journey into Bloomington

Two Sisters of the Holy Names and one of Holy Cross,
we rode by Greyhound, quick, safe,
dependable (and cheap):
three premises committed to the jolty roads
of contiguity and perpendicular sleep.

Your operator is... a fearful blank,
yet wheel in hand,
divided from his name,
he hurtled us through arbitrary hollows,
scholastic substance
in a joggled frame.

Some place near Kokomo,
where mileage mounts in smoke
and time goes off its standard,
we jerked and I awoke to four anachronisms:
two men with Samson hair, curled beards,
tall crowns and voluntary denim;
their women's faces paler than our own.

I watched them make a clearing
and gravely settle down,
the somber bonnets racked beside the hats,
and bundles of an inconclusive shape
hoisted beside our luggage overhead.

Aimed with gray look beyond me,
out of the close white cap,
one sentence in a language

that might have passed for dead
collided with compliance and forced me,
I confess, into bewildering
alliance by the accidents of dress.

Matinal

Four-thirty, morning. Unearthly time
by nuns' or any standard;
almost, this soggy May, monastic.
I close my door on sleep
for other sanctuary,
preceded by the birds
who long ago devised
their daylight saving.
Now, saving the daylight,
no other shape abroad
but the swinging step of rain
on rain-soaked turf.

Unbreakable as doom
five streetlamps watch me come
to keep my tryst.
Nailed each to a man-made cross,
usual as air,
we watch, mechanical,
dawnlight dispelling glare;
hooding our early brightness in a cloud
tempers the shock
and orders lonely emanations
by a clock.

Whitsunday Office

(heard for the first time in English)

Loosened, their tongues take fire.

If someone said, "I lift this weight of Latin,
dead for centuries, that you may sing,"
what hordes of murdered syllables would rise
to praise the God of Lauds and Vespers
in our prostrate days.

Well, somebody said. In choir I stand,
one with my sisters now at journey's end,
and hear, antiphonal, the chant break like a bell,
leap through the chapel vault,
spiral and somersault,
with here and there a crack
to make the music sweeter
for a happy fault.

Schooled in an ancient language, I've no word
to grieve its timely going.
Voices I had not heard
through reams of psalms on Sunday
revive and stir,
fragile as doves and whiter
on the morning air.

One glass the less to see through darkly
brings the image near.

From the Darkroom

The image comes up slowly where light fell,
Pure positive from what was only lack.
The figure in focus stamps the pale
Surrender of the broken seal.
Knowing the light, it gives light back,
Shadow and nuance till the vision's whole,
Shadow and substance from the quick
Delight in its reciprocal.

Deeper than death the image burns
Its counterclaim, unneutralized,
Renders detail in bold display
And will not, will not wash away
Or fix itself — the instant prized —
Against the lesson all love spurns.

FROM

When Sky Lets Go

Baroque Lament

Thistle. The name bleeds on the tongue
and the sessile leaves deny the curious
a handhold. These weeds are nature's mourning
for the unreclaimed. They flower profanely
on delivered ground and lift their passion
into regal attitudes.

Crowned with this wounding flare, the common lot
looks singular: light flows from secular stone
into a structure bleak as bone, and water dawns
over the dark root, to ignite the silken center
in the spiny shoot.

"Keep back!" the ranged barbarities decree
through kingdoms of the damned, crying unequal loss.
"What do you know of this crooked symmetry —
knowledge and love on the antique cross —
whose fingers dulled in canvas would intrude
upon the flower of my solitude?"

The Shell

My sealed house winters in its triple shell —
storm-windowed, weather-
stripped, and double-locked. I knock
icicles from the low eaves and watch the cold
come back cold
air condensing under doors. Sculptured carpet
snow below the cocomat. Once
I wanted that
blood too thick and hot
for comfort, all breath closer
than my own. Ice
forms again on the lintel, hardens
against the screen.

              In your light
sleep I pull back the drapes,
let the cold
light down, leave the flue open. Animal signs
of a long siege. Later
the barometer falls. Wind
hollows a track through the chimney. Casings
crack as they swell. The house
settles into the frozen ground.

In the Hellgate Wind

January ice drifts downriver
thirty years below the dizzy bridge. Careening traffic
past my narrow walk
tells me warm news of disaster. Sun lies
low, can't thaw my lips. I know
a handsbreadth farther down could freeze me solid
or dissolve me beyond reassembling.
Experts jostle my elbow.
They call my name.
My sleeves wear out from too much heart.

When I went back to pick up my life
the habit fit strangely. My hair escaped.
The Frigidaire worked hard while I slept my night
before the cold trip home.
Roots of that passage go deeper than a razor
can reach. Dead lights
in the station end access by rail.
I could stand still to fail the danger,
freeze a slash at a time, altitude for anesthetic.
Could follow my feet in the Hellgate wind
wherever the dance invites them.

The pure leap I cannot take stiffens downstream,
a millrace churned to murder.
The siren cries
at my wrist, flicks my throat, routine
as the river I cross over.

The Family Group

That Sunday at the zoo I understood the child
I never had would look like this: stiff-fingered
spastic hands, a steady drool, and eyes in cages
with a danger sign. I felt like stone myself
the ancient line curved inward in a sunblind
stare. My eyes were flat. Flat eyes for tanned
young couples with their picture-story kids.

Heads turned our way but you'd learned not to care.
You stood tall as Greek columns, weather-streaked
face bent toward the boy. I wanted to take his hand,
hallucinate a husband. He whimpered at my touch.
You watched me move away and grabbed my other
hand as much in love as pity for our land-
locked town. I heard the visionary rumor of the sea.

What holds the three of us together in my mind
is something no one planned. The chiseled look of mutes.
A window shut to keep out pain. Wooden blank
of doors. That stance the mallet might surprise if it
could strike the words we hoard for fears galloping
at night over moors through convoluted bone.
The strange uncertain rumor of the sea.

The Odd Woman

At parties I want to get even,
my pocket calculator rounds everything off,
taught to remember. I'm not so good
at numbers, feel awkward
as an upper plate without a partner.
Matched pairs float from the drawing board
into the drawing room, ears touched
with the right scent,
teeth and mouth perfect.

The cougar jaw yawns on the sofa back,
his molars an art-object.
The old and strange collect around me,
names I refuse pitched at my head
like haloes. This one is a dead ringer.
It rings dead. I pat the head of the beagle
nosing in my crotch and try to appear
grateful. A witch
would mount the nearest broom

and leave by the chimney. At ten I plot
my exit: gradual shift to the left,
a lunge toward the bourbon. The expert hunters
are gutting a deer
for the guest of honor. Soft eyes
accuse my headlights. I mention early
morning rituals. A colleague
offers to show me the door I've watched
for the last hour.

We come to my coat laid out
in the master bedroom, warm hands curled
in the pocket. I know
how a woman who leaves her purse behind
wants to be seduced. I hang mine
from the shoulder I cry on.
Say good-night to the Burmese buddha,
hunters in the snow,
and leave for the long river drive to town.

Letter to an Absent Son

It's right to call you son. That cursing alcoholic
is the god I married early before I really knew him:
spiked to his crossbeam bed, I've lasted thirty years.
Nails are my habit now. Without them I'm afraid.

At night I spider up the wall to hide in crevices
deeper than guilt. His hot breath smokes me out.
I fall and fall into the arms I bargained for,
sifting them cool as rain. A flower touch could tame me.
Bring me down that giant beam to lie submissive
in his fumbling clutch. One touch. Bad weather
moves indoors, a cyclone takes me.

How shall I find a shelter in the clouds, driven by
gods, gold breaking out of them everywhere?
Nothing is what it pretends. It gathers to a loss
of leaves and graves. Winter in the breath.
Your father looked like you, his dying proportioned
oddly to my breast. I boxed him in my plain pine
arms and let him take his ease just for a minute.

A Woman Possessed

her face blasted like a medieval weeper

GARCÍA LORCA

She remembered the charge.
A day like any other fall.
Her red shirt taunted dark shapes
in the street. The loud report
when that half-smile,
turned loose to goad the gusty animal,
stepped out to meet what waited.
She wanted to cast her body on the horns
of that forgetful season.
Black sounds hurtled from the chute.
The crowd looked on.

In that arena, narrowed to a skull
bone china shivered.
Clatter of Spode and Wedgwood
on mosaic tile.
The cameo relief of eyes glazed forward,
a crater where the trapped shale
burst its cone. Lava flowed
from thick veins into rock and there was more besides
the charred unknown
thin plates cracked
the sealed jar

on the grandstand shelf.
It may be, her reflexive feint
rushed the first dark lover,

proud blood in knotted streams. All night
the mad roar swelled
rain on the slack-limbed trees. Wet faces massed
on pavement. Nothing but this late fall.
It rumbled down on simple characters: a man
a legendary mount
a bull. Clay of their common drama
and the woman, old.

Psalm for a New Nun

My life was rescued like a bird from the fowler's snare.
It comes back singing tonight in my loosened hair

as I bend to the mirror in this contracted room
lit by the electric music of the comb.

With hair cropped close as a boy's, contained in a coif,
I let years make me forget what I had cut off.

Now the glass cannot compass my dark halo
and the frame censors the dense life it cannot follow.

Like strength restored in the temple this sweetness wells
quietly into tissues of abandoned cells;

better by as much as it is better to be
a woman, I feel this gradual urgency

till the comb snaps, the mirror widens, and the walls recede.
With head uncovered I am no longer afraid.

Broken is the snare and I am freed.
My help is in the name of the Lord who made
heaven and earth. Yes, earth.

Existing Light

for Lee Nye

A picture is worth a thousand words
of waiting. I thought I knew and waited
with the turn. The mirrors we were not
supposed to notice, circle my bedroom walls
to help me learn. In the corner of my closet
where that other black self hangs
praying for a pumpkin coach to cart away
the ashes of a prince, something lost or
spirited below, wakes up and stretches
in the early autumn sun, to let a loose wind
trifle with the veil. Outside, the fevered leaves
repeat my fall in choruses more ancient
than my own, and underneath the stairs
a guttural parrot calls tired
obscenities to a woman who lives alone.

I studied my unknown face in every opaque
glass, searched for the lie I kept
bottled in. Then you shot
with a focused eye to get inside
the compromising skin. Wherever the light
touched my body it left a bruise.
The bruise deepened to shadow, and shadow
flowed into shape. I felt my bones bend
against the vast concrete. Muscles
tell me what they were for in a dark
beginning of hope. Deftly you planned the angles
to cancel out reflections from my glasses.

Your strategies were natural and sure.
Light from a used sun flooded the street
where I stood, half woman, half nun, exposed.

Driving Home

The wheels keep pulling
toward that sunny sideroad.
I pull them back, headed for Blue Creek.
Grasses getting thin, the rushes lean. Nothing here
the wind can use against me.

In the long stretch
after Cataldo takes the hill, I think about
Clarence Worth Love's annulment
till a nerve gives way.
The gradual curve unwinds
the river again. Now it is green in the placid
crook of my arm
as the paired hands of those days
I wanted to die.

By the Superior exit
the highway crew leaves markers
I do not trust. The diamond
watch for crossing game, for ice and rocks,
hangs a legend on my lights.
I do the same. One star is out to get me.

A level sound. Pastures graze the trees
around the shoulder.
On a high beam, the mare swings
her dark side to the moon.
Something turns over in the trunk.
I think
one more time

of your black luggage
on the bed. I know
it may not carry me much longer.

Nights of flint and snow

fill with your long absence, the wind
not bitter,
ice an age to come. When sky lets go
it is warm work digging you out,
headlight cold in the socket,
one branch of the cedar
down.

    The compost path
steepens on both sides of the summer-
house. I think of old mines
reopened: veins of chard,
sad pods in coal-dark seams, the golden load
unfolding in the buried ear. I ride the waves
green, to the sea
warm rain.

        Weathered beets. The seal-faced kelp
torn from its rank salt bed
and the puckered kiss
of anemone.

        Water turns us back,
road and river curving under ice
to the deepening source. Home. Inside
your place is warm
plum and apple slowly turning wine.

With a Bottle of Blue Nun to All My Friends

1

Sisters,
The Blue Nun has eloped with one
of the Christian Brothers. They are living
in a B&B Motel just out of
Sacramento.

2

The Blue Nun works the late shift
in Denver. Her pierced ears
drip rubies
like the Sixth Wound.

3

This is to inform you
that the Blue Nun
will become Mayor of Missoula
in the new dispensation.
At fifty-eight she threw her starched coif
into the ring and was off to a late win
over Stetson and deerstalker,
homburg and humbug,
Church and State.

4

When you receive this you will know
that the Blue Nun
has blacked out

in a sleazy dive
outside San Francisco.
They remember her in Harlem.
She still carried her needle case
according to the ancient custom.

     5

You may have noticed
how the walls lean toward the river
where a veil of fog hides a sky diver's
pale descent. The parachute
surrounds her like a wimple.
That's what happens when Blue Nuns
bail out.
It's that simple.

Hope Diamonds

One hundred fifty miles down, these uncut
faces of stone drill toward light.
The odds in gravel and sand, one hundred million
to one. In Kimberley's basic rock, fourteen
million. Miners down on their luck call this
blue ground. Know the curse that follows thieves
and rich owners all the way back to the stolen eye
of an idol. Still they will work sixteen years
for a flash of that blue fire to polarize light,
believing the lode more than hard weight,
steel-blue in a self-inflicted wound. Or the captain's
greed that lowered a slave's dead body like a drowned
cat. They count on crystals fat as a fist
dug out with a penknife more than on carbon they burn
as they tunnel toward black lung.

                                    I suppose I could
learn to play oyster, coat minor irritations
with cultured pearls. Forget unbelievable pressures —
a million pounds to the square inch — and heat
too intense to imagine. Except for the unlucky shah
who died under torture refusing to give up the stone
of his father. The Brahman priest in exile. Or the star
of the Folies Bergères done in by a jealous lover.
The diamond brought from Lahore by Queen Victoria.
That Greek broker driven off a windy cliff with his wife
and sons. The mines near Pretoria. Consider Marie
Antoinette moving her jewels aside for the blade
and the gaudy American millionairess smuggled into

the harem to look, who paid by installment — first
money, then a husband gone mad and two children.

Recovery is rare at these levels, the shape of twin
pyramids touching bases more real than a wake.
The lure, the lore of the hidden. Every side
of refractory matter splitting light. Excited atoms
cooled to latticed arrangement. A deep
blaze waiting to surface. Bribe, ransom, dowry,
wage. The burning faces near as the constant desert.

FROM

Magpie on the Gallows

Slow-Motion Elegy for Kathy King

I roll the pebble of this word on my tongue, feel
the sting, the hard
salt taste of it. They never get it straight.
No way to splice the reel of wreck
and exile, the silent
film. You have passed on
to life in that cloudy home, leaving your friends
weighed down, shortening days
without you.

        Into the world, into the cloister
and out before me: whatever the future held
you held it first. Two sides of an old oak door
we traded supervision during lunch
and startled high-school seniors with our French.
That year the enemy who struck you down
enlarged your heart. How soon these summer
reruns make me sad.

        Twelve months in bed and you were
back mountain-climbing stairs.
To think I envied you the sound track
fading out, the rest.
A walk-on strangler found the fire escape and broke
your dormitory sleep.
You said it was a shortcut
to a private room, the violence you dreamed
locked in by a double door.

I saw it mirrored there.
Left behind, trying to name this
anger, this more-than-morning sickness, I interrogate
the tide. When you were mugged
police said, Do you still believe in civil rights?
A terrible neighborhood: They didn't ask you twice.
I watch you moving in to stay. Your brave words
skipping stones farther out than mine. Now they are
going down, coral and skull to lime.

If I could
match that other orator, the sea, I'd rage
out of bounds, beat the rock
you threatened. Lashed to the mast but never tied
to the script. No child
wearing a halo
ladles the ocean into this hole at my feet. A tourist
stalking elegant cuisine
appears to me. How easily the mind snaps
shut on itself, a razor clam.

How shall I know
the changing woman I am: the hermit crab scrawling
a private code. Dolphin, smart and playful,
towing a man-size brain. The killer whale spouting
news of deep water. Nothing's
the right matter. These waves break over me
and break again.

Portofino

Why, on this wine —
drenched reef of wind
and palm, of wave
and pine, do I recall
black coat and tails,
white vest, the singing
past, and a finch
pressed flat as a leaf
turned gold in the fall?

Extended Outlook

November days, and the vague shape of a wing,
of a claw at the sill, at the drawn
shade of the bedroom,
signals the oncoming freeze. Setting
the scent-baited trap for the shadow mouse
back of the dark pine cabinet,
the tenant hears the cat downstairs
whining to be let in.

               The tree is a violin bow
scraping the sound box of the house
all day. Close to the ribbed
breath, the scrolled end of wind under the eaves
turns back on the fine-tuned neck,
answers the shrill
jay in the caterwaul of blue
and failing light.

               Trying to score this weather
for strings, no hurricane, but a planned
diminuendo, I pretend that the house is my own;
the cat, my pet. That Canada
wishes me well. That the blue shriek and the wail
are a cradlesong and the gulf
repeating this gale in my ear, is an old friend
or no friend of mine.

Hanging the Pictures

Every day I hang a different picture. They are
mostly the same — Vermeer's girl
in blue turban — a woman, clothed or not,
looks from the matte into distance, the first time
knowing her name.

               What holds together or binds:
syllables roll on the tongue. No matter
how late, how ordinary or not, the given
covers the rapt body, wine-colored dress — Dolce —
lowered into light.

               Figures assume a shape she has
always practiced, cat and cricket shut out
where sleep cannot touch them. The other night,
good luck in the house, I killed a cricket, the second
one got away.

               The left-handed woman whose thought
is awash on my wall, and the tree that is always a woman
held in the storm's wake, a sky
not her own and larger, they are the same white
body of the charcoal nude who brings back the strait

and the water's precision, gradually louder, lapping
ashore. I drive two nails into wood to hang her.
On the floor Modigliani's red-haired woman
falls forward into the room's frame and a black
leap I recognize but cannot stop from singing.

The day you were leaving

the lock stuck on the attic door,
a bolt slipped into gear
for the last act, the forked dark
under the rafters
closed on itself. I took to my bed,
ice pack heavy on lids
as shells driven through holes in the skull
or weight slung from crossed winter limbs.
Someone who put on
my old voice from a drained throat
said lines you wanted to hear.
Smoke collapsed around hair that clung
to the brush. Ash drifted sill
and floor from trays
left to please empty themselves, the days
and the night you were leaving.

The Register

All night I hear the one-way door sigh outward
into billboard glare. The ninth-floor
cul-de-sac left by the wrecker's ball, my new
apartment.

        Inside the known hotel, décor of watered
silk and fleur-de-lis, the French Provincial
red-and-white, mine for the night, no more. A weak
bulb wears a halo through the dark.

                    The street
divides below the skid of rubber burning. One branch
leads to a hill's last word, one into morning.
Flying in place, hung from its thirst, hummingbird
in the honey throat of a flower.

                Bless me,
Father, I have sins to spare and love
these relics of the hybrid years I spent afraid
to move. Chant of common life, field lilies, all
that labor, too cautious then to spin.
Not even Solomon would know these regal lily flowers,
translated fleur-de-lis my wall
provides, the glory flowers-*de-luce*, of light breaking
clean on the iris. I open
my eyes to the light.

           Bless me, Father,
under heavy sun and hoping
still to make your life my own. I cannot nullify

the work this body's done
nor call each act religion. Wherever one road
joins another, blind, I think of you
and conjure up the loss. When two roads, gaining
speed, speed up to intersect, I cross
myself and lay the body down, arms open for what comes
to pass. Father, I am signing in.

Phobias Incorporated

Father Giuliano, the drama instructor, fainted
every time he saw blood.
When a nun in the class, newly acquainted
with stagecraft,
fed a hand to the band saw, Giuliano was the one
who had to be treated. My mother
applauded the hero.

            At the first clap of thunder,
she ran to the bureau for the rosary.
All through a stormy upbringing
under the kitchen sink after dark,
I repeated my lines. No wonder I link priest and parent,
twins in a Siamese startlement: Blood and Thunder,
Thunder and Blood. *Pray for us...*
at the hour of death.

            The real drama begins with
a thud — my sister — not claustrophobic, not
acrophobic, plunging from bed,
riding the nightmare bedrails. Her elevator shaft
endangered us all, marked women,
dumb waiters adrift on a sunken *Titanic.* Days
I rode up and down, wherever the tenants were going
for fun, not pushing the panic button.
I was afraid of cats.

            It's a circular story
and that's where I leave it: the Siamese leap
sucking breath, old wives'

tales, the alley cats my sister brought home
sheltered from storm,
early death of a hero and always
the drawn blood informing
our several lives.

Aladdin Lamp

With luck and the slow hand of the lover
I polish the lamp
to its antique glow. Over the ring of incised
rectangles where the double wick climbs
I watch the girl
dreaming by firelight. She plucks
the burning pitch from coals, lifts it high as a torch
and escapes the small brass picket fence
into the next century.

Nothing goes on but the fire. Swirls of opaque
roses caught in a slender chimney.
Clear at the heart of the globe's
Victorian shade
she runs with leaping tongues, the steady beat
of the track star. Small legs
pumping down the block
into the street where skaters gathered and past
the great beetle light of the tropics.

Wood spits in the andiron grate. What do apple logs
know, too old to catch fire? The pale observer
shudders from the cold room
toward the milky dawn of Chicago. She says,
If I kicked over the lantern would the man up late
notice? Already the hillside moon
lifts a gnarled trunk in its tongs. Hurricane
sweep of barn and town. Sky
in the window blazes.

Sanding the Chairs

All the way down to clean wood where the grain
shows hickory and a chair
is what stands after heavy lives settle in, and the housewives,
restless, sigh the spring
green, drying pale blue: dream Hollywood
in red enamel.

Every layer of paint, a country of wishes; the days
of townships lying in harbor
riding at anchor
follow the stars. And now, the women
lifted on domes of silence by musical chairs
glide over carpets to double duty
in the far bedroom.

The wrong feet on the rungs leave scars: they will
be gone when the fine dust settles.
Stripped down, legs tilted back in a bid
not to be tied to linoleum. Under the final coat,
bruise of buckle and clasp, the original
stain of the owner. For days
the curve of wood stays firm in the muscles.

Beetle Light

for Daniel Hillen

Hornets collect on the side of the sun.
Windows I cannot open
magnify their frames. Whatever beam insinuates
itself in squares I cut across
fades the color underfoot and turns my aim
deadly. Sitting by your shade, dreaming
stained blue light, I weigh New England
dark against my palm and peer
through bottle green, milky accumulations
of the night.

        Overhead, black light in the socket,
broken neck of bulb, the filament
connected like a nerve. Someone has tried to get rid
of the irremovable shade, a welder's gun
turned against a coffee tin. Nailed to the rude
beam; nothing will bring it down. I return to antique
brass, your art and mine, to kerosene,
candlelight, flash of battery and morning rays,
small at first, burning away
the fog.

        Bodies accumulate. Small flies repelled
by cold. Dusky millers
stupefied in glare. You watched them cross your palm
and kept their slight iridescence
mounted in the brain, wings free as forms your glass
borrows. I prefer bugs at a distance: in plates,

in print, because I am less violent behind a screen.
Britannica's hornet is sheer catharsis, a social
wasp, strikingly colored. The sting again.
Armed with a fly swatter, I watch one lift off the page,

begin to sing, the comb without the honey in the attic.
I darken toward the unexpected
spring. My plain-cooking landlady favors self-reliant
poets. They moon and thrive, trouble-free
tenants of the upper air. When I complain she mocks
the exterminator. Very soon they will die.

Picking Youngberries on Mr. Harvey's Land

Five hours by egg from noon, I am suing
my knees for support. The stretch
for the dark berry in a noose of morning glory
stains my hands, my jeans
bluer than heavenly pie through twined
thorn and I remember how the bear
hugged the woman
into another life in the park
for no reason.

Killer or lover, I would be sure of my clothes,
myself the blue intelligence
trapped in our capable bodies. Where
shall I leave these hands? Shall I give them
the studio rose, the cold
claws of dahlias shawled in blue air?
I am stained under glass, a choker
of vines like the green
housefall of the oak-leaf croton.

Hands go on their own errands: white bells
in the pail, berries
fallen in trenches. The long canes
and my arms arching. Sun
lowered into a dark bucket, a faraway eye
drowned in the scene. Together
we lift the known
interchangeable sweets, our underground
dreams to a nave of leaded light.

Keeping Up with the Signs

Meadowlarks nesting March to August yield
to summer traffic in the dovetailed grass.
Three clear notes. DO NOT WALK IN OPEN FIELD.

I run the way my feet suggest. Upheld
by ringing turf and larkspur flash, I chase
meadowlarks nesting. March to August yield

sways heavy on the cornstalked land I flailed
to find the spot where larks come less and less.
Three clear notes do not walk. In open field,

runways the wind lays flat, fill up. Revealed
in the natural clutch called happiness:
meadowlarks' nesting march to August yield

in the tilt of wind, rainswell and the cold
mating ground, to bed with the dangerous
three. Clear notes do not walk in open field.

I leave five clues for the field guide whose wild
speculation turns the head. Shells express
meadowlarks' nesting march to august yield.
Three clear notes do not. Walk in open field.

Gold Ring Triad

Cheerful as Martin of Tours dividing his cloak
with the beggar, my mother took that wide
souvenir from her finger to give me an equal share.
Her ragged sunflower face glowed with the brush
of her lover's hand, opened a space in air.
I ascended there, peered over fences of neighboring
yards, head half-turned to marauding
birds. Looked into the leashed
animal lives next door and a caucus of purple finches
campaigning against the cold. Already a chill
invades the old injury, the crooked knuckle stays

what's left of a double ring. With a narrower band, I
promised to marry no one, live for everyone
behind the high stone wall: it was a marriage in air,
no longer in that zone high above the clouds. My head
quivered, a severed and perilous freight. To steady
the wealth of my own ground, I trespassed outside
the gate. Imagine a squirrel, surefooted flagpole saint
sent into the closed fist of sky. Raffish
head, death's-head, the ongoing neck: how exposed
the staff that keeps us vertical!

                        In this replicated
sun I praise everything that fuses clay
and fire: earth broken and tilled,
the usual harrowing
sign of division. And I remember pain, confined
by my portion, waiting in the hospital bed
for the disk to mend. My body

worn so thin the ring slipped from my right hand
and fell unnoticed. At home
I missed that relic of two lives
I could never find again.

                    And you, my sister, my friend,
knew my grieving, gave me back the dead
woman's share. I wore it on the left, hand of true
marriage, pledge sinister. Relic of unions
blessed though not made in heaven, my poor
lost mother, almost a child bride. In the first
luster of final vows I tried to appear older, rub initials
smooth. Her half, profane
from the start, bore none: no Jesus, Mary, Joseph
to pillow the dying head.

                    It was destined to take me
elsewhere. I wear that ring in bars, in bed, wherever
it fits, the right little finger
beside the opal that is not my stone: half-lost
ring of my dead mother
forgiven, ring of abandoned lives
knit into my own.

FROM

The Light Station on Tillamook Rock

1. The Geologist's Map

Three laps farther right, I might have been
Mormon: born on the Idaho line where the valley
drains into Oregon. Two hundred million
years gone by, Ontario was the edge. I lean
toward the coast, the ballast
of an earlier life.

                At four I moved
west from the Snake winding north
to a country sprung from collision. Cut off
from her past, the continent drifted: bedrock
seafloor, ranges sheared on the bias
building a new margin.

                    Falling off edges, I
never did crawl. When I walked,
the world an unsteady place: California
shifting toward Alaska. Today's Steady Quake
Watcher from Newport Scans Wobbly World
by James Long. Face of my brother-in-law,
jaw twice as strong. I know these men,
the watchers: they will not
be moved, even by an earthquake.

                        It is to you
I speak. In five or ten million years, Portlanders
can wave, if you're right, to San Francisco
sliding past on its way to Juneau.
Trusting my feet, now that I've found them,
more than anything afloat or on wheels,

I would leave my imprint
on cement, on rock, or in a book
for the watcher of the future.

                                Walking sandy
shore, I admire my Nike herringbone
beside the waffle-stomper tread, the wider
radials of cars advancing toward
reverse conclusions, and the barefoot print
I can't identify as girl or gull.
Not to mention the peculiar
tread, unchained, the ocean leaves, receding
from its bed.

                        Features of the earthquake map:
Africa slowly turning left,
the Mediterranean squeezed into a puddle.
Long ago the Himalayas rose in a cosmic
fender-bender. While California
drifts, the geologic fidget of Puget Sound
and Northwest Oregon, caught as we've always
known, in the middle, reminds us how
the region's better part is drawn
eerily quiet.

II. Power Failure

Walking the shore, Augustine hoped to comprehend
the mystery: darkness welling up to fill
a small depression hollowed out of sand. Being
fond of light — and secrets — I understand
the impulse: the will to know, the wish to be
turned back.

        Mind turns back on itself: flood-
waters recede. What came to light
last week swims farther down. Unscientific as
the television sounds, that experienced
beachcomber frightens me. Flotsam we ignore,
he says, will not return until four years
have passed. I carry pen and paper
as others carry mace.

        My retrieval system
isn't working right. Blame it
on weather, heavy skies. When I'm in bed,
a sailboat heeling over
keels above my head. I can't recall the name.
Centuries of obscurity. All that time,
scientists declare:

        The atmosphere forgets
its past every two weeks. East and west,
those are the breaks. Later, when it doesn't
matter, the legend flashes on
the screen: *Submarine volcano forms an island.*
Island gives way to water. Experts say

Crater Lake may be losing its clarity.
All the same, I float to meet my past, hoping
the mist will rise.

IV. Sounding the Ocean

I have invited the sea into my windswept room,
made the ocean my library,
its bays and shelves, dim carrels in the rock.
The winds I hear
speak volumes, storms that wrack the shore:
the ocean giving up, not
giving up its dead.

         I look for them in pools
and estuaries, some cunning
fragment of an eardrum's anchor
the wild surf beats until it looks like shell
I pick up on the beach, honey-
combed by parasitic sponge: I can no longer
tell its origin.

        That old siren song
to the north. Bad weather
rolls across the waves. Cape Flattery to Cape
Disappointment and out sixty miles — the long
configuration of the coast that drives
the crabber and the salmon-fisher's boat
to hull-strewn graves.

        The silence of the deep
sea is a legend water writes
on water when the mind is still and wind
escapes the city streets,
roaming desert flats we populate with stars,
thick as our fancies. Oceanographers

know better: their echo-sounding given back
at shifting levels, reveals a phantom floor:
squid, fish, or small planktonic
shrimp. The layer moves, vertical migrations
keyed to light and dark.

      Diatoms sift down
like snow: manna for the deep-sea
creatures — tiny shrimp, one claw enlarged
to stun its victim, clacking
the joints of that sea-based weapon.
Nothing is ever wasted in the sea. Ocean is
a good provider: minute
relics of the smaller dead — shells, skeletons,

souvenirs of cycled and recycled matter. That
astonishing red carpet, rolled out
in the diver's memory, its only jewels, sharks'
teeth and the earbones of whales.
Chemical salts, trace metals — iron, cobalt,
nickel, copper, gold.
Drift of volcanic dust and Arctic Ocean ice-
pack. River silt and silica. Fall of meteoric
debris.

    Like a tree crashing in unlit forest,
the sea, viewed in another light,
emits no sound. Only its bonds cry out: shoal
and promontory, cliff, island, fissure, reef.
Lacking noisy tenants, barriers,
and weather, water seeks its own level, water
holds its peace.

v. The Return from New England

Coming back, I walk the beach, the offshore
road, ear quickened to the shells
that amplify and fall into a former
litany: clack of Clackamas and Estacada.
Softer syllables of plants
spilling over banks and gullies. *O all ye*
holy succulents and sages, We beseech thee,
hear us.

     Oregon grape, barley, Scotch broom,
clover, lupine, thimbleberry, laurel,
morning glory, heather, Canterbury bells. All
that is vaguely Latin
trembles in these shoots. I am breathing
the air of an old benediction. Memory
pulls at the Latin roots. *O escalonia,*
Spanish cousin, flowering hedge,
whose other name is saxifrage. *We beseech*
thee, hear us.

     In a world of fixed
responses, these are the rain's gift,
salt air celebration. Calla lilies, our name
for Sisters of Providence, as in Divine,
growing wild in Marshfield, later called
Coos Bay.

     The Coast Range falls away,
Cascades, the old declared
dead, every mountaintop another story: Hood

where I toasted retreat from the crowd.
The dome of Holy Names: still life of a nun
framed in the studio window. Adams,
rounded at the cone, the Northwest ice-cream
ad. Saint Helens, restless sleeper.

O all ye
saintly conifers and creepers. We beseech thee,
hear us.

On my knees before the fire, the wood
too green, I feed *New Yorker* pages
to the coals and watch
that elegant four-color blaze: Wedgwood-and-
Tanqueray fire, Christian Dior,
smoke of Royal Copenhagen, Glenlivet fire
and *Eau Sauvage*. Why is it the news
glows with such passion as the margins darken,
the words dissolve, and ashes
creep along the edge?

vi. Breaching the Rock

Pacific, the true misnomer: around the Columbia
Bar, old salts from Singapore
to London and Seattle recognize some namer's
private joke on the unsuspecting.
The Rock falls plumb into those storied combers:
240 feet of ocean pool
the summer whales frequent to rub off barnacles
against basalt. They dive, cavort, spout freely
without concussion.

           Old-timers took the mission
with more than a grain of salt.
They'd seen their cronies drowned in harebrained
schemes to tame the Rock. This expert,
hired and fired-up by the government, this crazy
builder, Charles Ballantyne,
was predictable hearts-and-flowers. Fishermen
knew the wiles of Terrible Tilly, let him learn
on his own.

           Discouraged, the builder fanned out
over the countryside to sign
eight stonemen, innocent of town gossip. Found
the right place to keep them
willing. Seasonal gales had set in early. Talk
was cheap as a beer in every saloon.
Across the river, Cape Disappointment loomed,
the keeper absent, and the skeleton
crew rehearsed in reticence.

Twenty-six days of
Disappointment — checkers, whodunits,
and chess — the quarrymen cheered for the revenue
cutter, danger better than this.
Near the Rock, the sea saw their mistake: waves
rampaging, ship astride, cutter
moored to planted buoy, small boat over the side
where Ocean turned to Buffalo Express
stampeding into *Killamuck* Station, into a narrow
cleft.

Six hours nearer dark they'd landed four
and terrified the others, mainly one
Gruber, 300 pounds or 21 stone of quivering fat,
too big for his breeches buoy. The hoodoo
light guttered ahead. Wiser Indians' celebrated
Land of Many Waters, most of them dangerous,
railroaded the frightened masons back to the old
Disappointment, ready for chess and survival,
ready to settle for less.

ix. The Columbarium: Everlasting Consideration

How shall we market death? Not that loved one,
faithful dog-at-heel, not the bird-in-hand
worth two, the boa close as a collar,
not the son we married off, the husband
underground before he makes it to the top. We
market the only real — the Self
ensconced in the dome's dark lantern. We tell
our client, Frankly, there is no caretaker
like the cold, considered sea.

                                 No visitors who
can't afford the chartered helicopter, no heirs
greedy for sterling and china, no survivors
gloating. Absolute satisfaction
or your money back. No vandals, ritual grave
robbers, no hard-up medical students, artists-
in-anatomy. You owe it to yourself:
your ashes perfectly safe. Eternity-at-sea:
How beautiful! Starts at six-ninety. Urns
encased in Plexiglas. The dead

                                   secure beyond
belief. Fees will rise: one- to three-thousand
next year. Buy now, move in
later. Only 467 thousand slots. If you're not
a dead star and would like to be
considered for the best spot of all, a founding
member, call today. The Hollywood Hall of Fame
and twenty-five grand on the line

bring a niche in the lantern room. Eternity at
sea. How many pearl divers,

                              air travelers, dory
fishermen, mutineers, suicides,
sad captains, and cruising wives, no longer soft
to the touch, have made it there for less.

XII. Geography as Warning

The wildcat drilling started in 1919, the year
of my birth. The legend grows. Where
then, was Lion Rock, two feet
offshore, the name a halo and the claws
retracted as if something more could be expected
of the sleeping form
the ocean gives a voice? An active coastline —
land, risen; or sea level, dropped: swales,
breaker bars and scarps. The fracture
zones. At the bottom of a bay
lies the Millicoma floodplain, Morphic river-
tongues in thousands, whose meaning
no one knows.

The Seaside Nat, circa 1928.
In the heated pool I stroked away ocean shock,
my heart developing a slight
murmur. Even then Pacific waters meant a mutual
embrace. Rockaway at ten, starfish
clinging to the rocks we balanced on. Black gym
bloomers, sailor blouse, knit beret: I
am the younger version of those boaters, argyles
and golf knickers; women in short
skirts and slingback shoes, there on the putting
green.

Later, Agate Beach, white-ribbon stone
cut and polished for my first ring.
Newport and rhododendron. Bandon in April, wind
an evil force. Abandoned by a traveling

superior who planned this Arctic curse, an early
spring picnic, we shivered
by a three-foot wall until, at five, our driver
back, we were delivered
to our winter home.

Gearhart, our isolated
summer place. Old nuns and sickly younger ones
kept busy those strong enough to work.
Mid-forties, then, we sneaked in twenties bathing
suits, out the back door, over the hill,
to reappear as tourists, believing they couldn't
tell. Medieval costumes, a giveaway,
not to mention white arms and whiter legs.
Limbs, an old nun called them. "I'd like a
limb of lamb," on Saturday.

Next, Lincoln City:
holiday on the fringe. Writing up a storm
through that perfect week, the disk
mending slowly. Years after, balanced between
out and in, and ready for the perfect
ending, a trip to Neah Bay, I saw our friend,
Skipper, slam the car door on his index
finger and sweated out the day. The old wounds
open like anemones. We
pray them shut.

The names float like buoys of
every kind — lighted whistle, spar
buoy, can, nun buoy, bell, and we are on our
knees again, map spread out like comics:

                                        Cape
Sebastian where the arrows fell. *O all ye canny*
mariners and martyrs, Pray for us. O
all ye terrors lurking off the coast, Pray
for us. O all ye inland patrons of the lost,
Ora pro nobis.

              Cape Lookout mapped as a dagger,
Pray for us. Cape Perpetua
gored by wild beasts, *Pray for us.* Cape Shoal-
water, Cape Foulweather, Destruction
Island, Camp Castaway, *Spare us*
O Lord.

           Cannibal Mountain, Butcherknife Creek,
Turnagain Arm, Quicksand Bay, Devils
Churn, Spouting Horn, Boiler Bay, *Turn not away*
Your Face from us, Hear us, O Lord,
Have mercy.

            The oceanic floor: anatomy becomes
familiar as the forms we walk inside.
Wrecks containing treasure, the flowering skull.

xvi. Counting the Winter Dead

Off the Oregon coast, thirty-three in storm and sudden
squall. Fifteen boats gone down.
Where do they lead: risks the gill-netters take
gambling hard lives against the waves,
skill against the tide? If hands on the tiller
shake, let Valéry sing
their ashes to rest in vaults of Tillamook Light
turned Columbary-by-the-Sea.

                              Turn back, sad
fisherman, we might have said, before the last
wave finds you with your
proud back turned. The ocean knocked at cabin
windows. Water followed you inside
your second skin. You were alone, we know.
The rest is guesswork and a corpse
washed in. The suit you called survival
made a shroud.

The Mary Jean, Inez, the Merrimac, the Oregon
Otter. *Spare us, O Lord!*
O all ye vessels, plying wild water, Spare us!
O all ye fishers of the deep:
The Annie B, the Frank, the Sean, Christina J,
Mariah and Aloha, the mythmaking Cygnet,
O every underwater magnet,
drawing to our doom, Parce nobis, Domine!

The Debonair, Sagacious, the Odyssey, Avenger,
We beseech thee for a sign! Rangers

off the headlands, *O all ye*
watchers of the sky and scanners of the wave!
O every creature
voracious and benign, Spare us O Lord!

xvii. The Book of Sediments

Eye is an ocean bounded on every side by desert,
the salt shore framing the wide
salt sea. Mourning on land, I've the drooping
habit of weeping willow. Mid-Pacific
tears are rain, stunning the oysters open: seed
the ancients held
responsible for pearls. On my nightstand

lamplight glows, a glass base filled with shells
containing news of ocean. If the shell encloses
what the sea says to the listener,
every whorl and coil reveals the secrets there.
Down the long evolutionary avenues, some random
turning called the Veiled
Pacific Chiton and knew the walled slow way

the embryo, even then, was tending. Chiton-like,
an armadillo of the sea,
I grew a shell before I went to school.
Though water is my element I cannot relax in it:
where is he now — father, messiah, lifeguard,
unburnished lover and friend — who, more than any
other, believed in the lost
free-swimming self?

                    Waterborne among the common
Scorpio Conchs, I search the hard way
back. Attached to wharves and rocks I recognize
the blue mussels and cling to the sources
of a truer life. The sea is a source. Consider

the subterfuges of the sea: the scallop's
myriad eyes, poison of cones, dark dye of squid,
anchor thread and cuttlebone.

                              Given the choice
between toothpaste and ink, I know
where my loyalties lie. The rarer False Scorpio
Conch, for a while believed not to exist,
acknowledged at last: my reminder of everything
flawed. In the imperfect tropics,
venom matches paradise: not even heaven secure.
If I called you now

                          unsure over darkening waters
would you hear me? In the shy littoral
snail, I follow the clockwise coiling of shells,
admiring clumsy clams and sedentary
oysters. You imagined yourself at night tossing
your tired body, the unsteady heart
in your chest, over the riverbank into flotillas
of sleep.

          At midnight, startled awake, I see my
self adrift on the vast dark,
the raft Kon-tiki, the night lights on: the pale
moon jelly Aurelia swaying the chains
of a bright arcade, going where wind and waves
take me. Balsa logs,
bamboo hut, my frail shelter, the exact analogue
for the universal voyage.

                    The darker the night,
the more life pressed around us. Bold survivors
embroider a theme of hunger and pursuit,

the phosphorescent, bug-eyed creatures rising up
from the unknown deep. Shadowy
gulls hover over silver-sided fish flashing past
to safer waters, disappear
in the predatory swoop as though sparks of Roman
candles.

       Ship Harbor Inn — high above the Sound
we slept while frogs and crickets made
a fluttering circle on the ear's horizon. Heard
one long note, the foghorn cutting
in and out of sleep. Like waves we know our ore
by weight. Neatly we sort out beds of separate
deposits: gold from monazite, red
garnet from zircon. Disaster always in our wake,
we stumble on, sifting platinum

                from chromite,
grain by grain. Some regard the ocean prospect,
make themselves minor prophets; others have gone
for broke. Isn't that Gruber there,
the 300-pound quarryman we left, too fat
to fit in, refusing to be tied? His midsection
circled by two life preservers, he made it over,
the first to pass dry-shod.

       Sun-drenched sepals
in the old stereoscope: two complementary views
(right eye and left) on film the brain
registers and light fuses to a third dimension.
In this one, the ferry's docking at Shaw Island:
a brown-robed nun in pillbox hat
with veil attached, runs down

the gangplank. Clank of heavy chains, and then,
double dissolve into Friday

                              Harbor Whale Museum,
where we saw a brain three times our size.
Remember the days we took to let the sea settle?
Bald Hill and Dinner Island? Cape San Juan
and Sunset Point. I tried the public
telephone: a killer whale was on the line. Off
the hook, a foreign body, flailing, broke
through undreamed light and water.

FROM

Imaginary Ancestors

Stages of Family Life

My mother, the prima donna in the family
opera, conducted herself
like Callas. Stories she told were fabricated
from whole cloth, the fibers
synthetic. Not knowing your past could be
the shortest cut to a self-made
woman, Mother said, as she put her shoulder
to the wheel, believing she had
invented it.

        Through every crack in the door,
a grand entrance. For the least
innocent question, an oratorio. Clichés
drained from her hourglass,
precise as three-minute eggs, then turned
upside down to start over. She thought of
the word as a bird in the hand
worth two in the aria. Each random complaint
provoked a recitative:

                starving Armenians
camped at the edge of our plates
waiting for handouts. Adrift in the city,
the ghost of Horatio Alger
bound to win decorated our mantelpiece
propped between ships coming in.
She filled the uncertain rest of her past with
trills and cadenzas. We remembered
our roles:

My brother, the bad one, pledged
to upstage her. My sister, the pretty one,
chose a doll for a diva. Our peace-
loving bookkeeping father still
lived in the garden. And I, the reliable
smart one, trained my lorgnette
on the happiest scene, mere words no excuse
for the music in that burst
of elaborate dying.

Honesty

Money doesn't grow on trees, my mother said,
leaving out the dollar plant
dried in the Goldmarks' garden. All winter long
it was my pocketbook,
thin membrane laminating seeds
that could be counted. Everyone else said Money
or Honesty. Mother rode trolleys,
waited for the stage.

That was the year her face flattened. Toward the cement
plant, the mint stretched
to the river. Crushed, it smelled like a letter
from Grandma, the one we never met.
Silver-haired and always
sending candy, she was my secret redeemer.
My brother said she hated the pope, Peter's bark
worse than Eve's famous bite.

We're not made of money, Mother said, and Grandma
shipped crates of oranges
that grow largely in California. *The Book of Knowledge*
showed *Lunaria*, tall with a silvery septum,
called it everlasting.
I wrote it all down, hidden in the chest
with my underwear. Summers at Rockaway, I collected
sand dollars.

> *Moonwort*, I said. Dipping my toes
in water I waited for incoming tide.

Grandmother Grant

Not the rejected lies of the New York Foundling
home, not the adoptive widow of two names,
one of devious spelling,
not the dog tag pinned to the plaid dress
for the train ride to Missouri, but the surname
worn like a shoulder brand
on the skin of the natural mother,
Grandmother Grant.

When I went in my black robes through the hot
streets of the city, a young nun
pale as the star I followed
led to the desk of a three-faced guardian. One
face called me Sister to my face. One was
motherly, "Oh my dear, I can't risk the wrong
information." One, older than the order, nervous,
bit the sentence off
on a fragment of Irish history.

I couldn't get past the gate. I recognized
the road I was on
led to heaven or hell. Either was barred,
date too early for the name,
a Closed File. I should tell my mother to come.
Back home in Oregon, sixty-nine, wanting to know,
not wanting to know, she waited.
I crossed the continent angry, three thousand
miles of featureless plain.

Mother, now that you're gone, I'm the same,
swaddled no more in the habit.
Whatever it is that drives us — bad blood,
the face in the unlighted window,
I'm bound to get it straight. If he knocked her down
in the stinking hold of a ship and raped her,
if she followed him out of the church
into the oldest garden under moonstone limbs
of the sycamore, it's too late
to cover her tracks.

        Whoever she was, whatever ties,
here is my claim. I need to come into my own.

On My Father's Side

Off the coast of Council Bluffs, Great-Grandfather's
ocean liner went down. Years before
he sailed into the plan of God
Mother was already waving. She knew his ship
would come in, another miracle. I studied
the map of my head, painted the hull
orange. The mainsail was blue
over musical water. Nobody understood
how I fell heir to
the size of his hands like my father's.

All night in my head going down, the sea-keen
of his wake. I wrote his lament in the book
covered with envelope linings.
No one in this family can carry a tune, Mother said,
and I carried it to the attic. Safe there,
I threw my rag doll
a life preserver in the flood of infallible
pronouncements. My father's father's father's voice
rolled like the sea
through my father's impossible speech.

Clare of Assisi

Far ahead, we could already make out the bishop
on his way to our parish. Confirmation
time, time to choose one more saint
to protect us. I settled on *Colette,* but my
copycat friends followed suit, and those
carbon Colettes were too common.

                         In secret
I transferred to *Clare,* pleased to honor
Clarence, my father: a name so clear
it signaled the onset of trumpets or Shakespeare's
flourish of hautboys, the clarion
sweetly confused in my mind with a carillon.

Then it was bells followed me everywhere, chimed
through the night-deep waters of
drowned cathedrals. Bells transmuted to birds
singing *Poor Clare, Poor Clare,* all through
the early light where the maiden walked
barefoot, spirit-sister to Francis, *Francis,*
my own bad brother's second of three
given names.

                Clare ran away when they
wanted her married, changed at the church door
her sumptuous clothing for sackcloth
and, shorn of her hair, clung to the altar when
relatives came to drag her away. Clare
carried the day.

        I carried her name but shrank
from the unwashed poor. I wanted them
shaven and showered with clean underwear. I
wanted them nice. At the New York Passport
Agency, I took the official
advice: *Drop everything but the Madeline.*
You'll save yourself

              all kinds of trouble. I
saved myself. Chopped off the Mary,
axed out the Clare, forgot about burlap and
beggars, let go of the altar. Assisi was a lot
like Camelot, as hard to forget.
With ocean and lake everywhere, I still
hear those bells under water.

Gilbert of Sempringham

Plain Gilbert to me, who wore with a heavy veil
the luckless name let down by a bishop
on my shorn head. "Henceforth you will be known as
Gilbert," the same given first
to a New York nun in an extant grave, who wrote
Our Nation's Builders, stacked
in the classroom cupboard.

The fifth grade clapped when I came. "Sister, did you
write this book?" their eyes bigger than the words
inside. I shook my head, refusing to claim
that honor, showed them the dictionary. The books
never wore out, their blocks
longer than chapters I learned to translate
a paragraph at a time.

Gilbert, my saint, if I had you my own, always
in the shadow of the great. "The real
Sister Gilbert was a saint, was she your aunt?"
Should I tell them I hated the murky lines? They quoted
her life of the foundress, room gone in the haze
of Mother Mary Rose. I tried
and the fifth grade was right.

O my English patron, believe I drew water from your
twelfth-century springs.
Only the Gilbertines survived, your order
of nuns, not the men
you gave them as masters; those and the crumbs

you scraped from refectory tables,
pledged to discourage waste.

I gave you the frugal ways of my imitative life.
How could I follow you, founder,
lost as I was with my foundling mother, starved
ghost of my convert father,
under a shroud at sixteen in all weathers, white
body lost in heat,
not even my name new-borne?

The Woman with Fabled Hair

In the life to come I unravel and let down
the extravagant bolt of hair,
the braids of a saint caught in silk
all the days I remember. Cut free of the tin box
the future crown is always mine. Repeated
shocks of auburn, shades of my mother's
upswept hair when she ran away
with the man who would fade to my father.

I am waiting for him to come again, the simple
man in elaborate disguise, wearing his
bones like a prophet. When enough time has been
lost, her hair will fall to my shoulder.
Dense folds released from the veil, this past
woman's glory recovered
brings back the forgotten blend, lilac and
amber, cypress and plum.

The man will look into my eyes when I come
for the girl in the glass, the one to be
lifted down from the wall where she hangs
in the white dress, the too-short curls. "We have
plenty of time," taking the girl's right hand.
"We have from now on," stroking the nails
she tried to press down, kissing them. He won't mind
that her teeth are set far apart,

believing that passionate sign. *Don't be afraid,*
and the brain in its time carries her
over the doorstep, engraved words to a bride.

These forevers that keep
disappearing, bureau drawers of a life
that threatens to move us out. The body
meets the animal it ran from: dark bush
parted in the night, wet fur, the cave lighted
by the eyes of lynx, my own
dense longing.

Ulysses S. Grant (1822–1885)

The Treasury voted nine to one against your ordinary
chin, though you cut mustache
and beard to sit for the profile photo. With Liberty,
that noble woman, your dreams of fame were half-
dollars, the silver part
aristocrat like millionaires of Boston Common,
the homespun sage of almanacs, obverse
eagles and bells.

       More than the rest, Mother believed
blood tells but wouldn't say what. She
claimed you — with or beyond reason — saving the penciled
Mary Grant pinned to the front of her faded plaid
like an heirloom. I read available
histories, imagined Army tanks of social disease
rolling down, a plague on my doorstep. Expected my mind
to go off, the slow tongue
fused by drink and vague neglect.

       Under the West Point
manners and epaulets, beat the timid heart of a store-
keeper. I joined your campaign against migraine,
kissed your clay feet warm, hung over
the bedpost, head split clean as rails of your honeymoon
cabin. In Mother's kodak, Dad stands in knee-length
coat, starched shirt and hat, one hand on a post,
stunned by the history he's come into.

       On the back
in Mother's cursive hand, a legend of relationship

to Julia Dent, Grant's First Lady.
It makes no sense without a double tie, adoptive
mother and real in league
to right some kinsman's wild throw. *Little pitchers
have big ears*, Mother says, and so
the story closes. I watch the smoke from a president's
quota — twenty cigars a day — ticket

                                        to cancer of the throat
and memoirs written, dying. A family man to the end
he sold his life for wife and children. Even now
the overheard alarms. Mother died of a perfect heart
tracking invented lives through the land, the record
always partial. I look for her nine-years' grave
through a light sifting of snow, travel cold
as she lies without a coat of arms.

Galileo's Case Reopened (1564–1642)

Lie still, son Galileo, while we crack
the seal, undo the nails and let the bronze
repeal of history correct your bones.
And what's three hundred years, the long trajec-
tories of moons, their lines crisscrossing like
a pinball game? Believe me, no one wins
without a slight distortion of the lens
changing the curve of inference and luck.

Timely as rockets bursting on the mind's
black earth, I plant the fleurs-de-lis of kings
over your grave to mark the faithful skull.
Inside the socket where the globe unwinds,
the shaken bell of every iris rings,
your brain flowers like a solar model.

Sister Maria Celeste, Galileo's Daughter, Writes to a Friend

Again I am at sea. If this be faith, it is not
the faith I bargained for
when I gave that troubled half-life over; the slow
sidereal day in trade for a guarantee
the drift persuades me to consider.

                      This morning
lifting the shipboard cup from my lips into the hands
of my judges, the cheap wine cloying my tongue,
I see the rift clearly. Nothing — not words, the unlikely
notice of scholars, not the face
set toward a cruciform sun; least of all, the ritual
meant to distract us — eases this passage.

                         I have
bargained everything away for the slow word, hard
as science, for an uncertain page
in the text of the future. Have taken in vain
the name of God's mother, coupled it with foreshortened
heaven. This is my home
voyage, too fast to be wasted in anger.

                        Call me a vessel
come in from the peaks and valleys written in water.
Blot out my name. Moored to my own
tilted deck, I ride, I am riding
the battered hulk to the ocean floor.

Modern Primitives

Whether the woman carry a waterpot on her head
deforming her skull; whether her feet
be bound in the cradle to keep
dainty steps from straying; whether the earlobes
sag with her husband's gold; or her waist contract
to the span of Victorian corsets,
these urges to mutilate ourselves follow us
everywhere. We invoke tribal custom, beauty,
rites of initiation, health, and religion
as we torture our bodies, the need
more severe, it is said, among primitives. One
other motive remains: to punish,
and what more efficient than asking the law-
breaker to punish herself?

                    When my father made a
fist of his firm right hand, flexing
his muscle, the small tattoo
ballooned to a legend — *C.C. Defrees* — scrolled in
blue on his upper arm. It didn't say
Notary Public, but it could have. Oh, he was a
marked and remarkable man! Our fingers
traced the salmon-colored border. *Daddy, do it
again!* The man who ordered that
modest tattoo wasn't the soft-spoken father
we knew, though he could be
reckless with nickels at the slot machines
in the bus depot.

Dusting her nose with a powder
puff, my mother quoted Sir John Davies
whom she hadn't heard of: *Beauty's only skin-deep.*
At the time, she was opposed to
the hard stuff: rouge, lipstick, mascara.
Worst of all, hair-dye, the work of the devil, no
daughter of hers, et cetera.
When I was stubborn — that is, almost always — my
father said, *She's hardheaded, she was brought up
on goat's milk.* In contests with my sister
I proved it again and again,
banging my skull with books, almost
to concussion.

Years later, the eye doctor said,
You have a fixed pupil. What happened?
I couldn't recall. *Never a dull
blow to the head?* In the convent, an eager pupil,
I studied the lives of saints
who walked with pebbles in their shoes,
wore hair shirts and crowns
of thorn. Deathless lines in my head, I limped
along, born to two noble callings.
Even now — at large and briefly immortal — I flog
myself with gilt-tipped
scourges, lie on a bed of rushes, vowed to be
better than good.

The Giraffe Women of Burma

Their voices reach us as if from the shaft
of a well, these long-necked
women of Padaung, whose clavicles, depressed
by all that brass, reveal
the burden of beauty. Over the miles, the years,
I shoulder the weight, embrace the wood
of our common cross, and under the load,
the scars, these bold
striations.

      Slung from my neck, the brass-bordered
crucifix like the ring on my hand
recalled an earlier day when priest and medicine man
shaped the first coil for the five-year-old
with fiery promise and a flash of metal. Then
divination with relics, with chicken bones
for the favored time. Protection from tiger bites,
one legend says, and I feel the stripes
change subtly

      as elders rehearse the punishment
for adultery. The necklace of habit removed,
atrophied muscles let go
and the light-headed woman surrenders her weight
to a coffin. Meanwhile, these ringing
tiers and silver chains, coins
swung from the links, tell the world
who these women are, identify their tribe. Legs
shackled with brass

or held in place by detailed
prescriptions, reduce their walk
to a hobble. The pillow under the chin does not
spell comfort, but elegance
in position. They cannot tilt the head back
to drink sweet water, must bow to sip
from a straw. If they set their ornaments aside,
against the tribal law, they need
a brace or the hand of a friend, merely
to keep on breathing.

          In a Rangoon hospital, X rays
screen the skeletal change: collarbone
shoved down, ribs displaced, a neck
that, year by year, looks
longer. The downward pressure on the spine
means something has to give. All through the blank
December I chose unfrocking, my one
alternative, I held my head carefully
above the collar,

         folded the turtleneck twice
in a mockery of survival. My lungs filled
with water, closing. Whatever raises this voice
from a long way down
lies close to you as air. Help me to hold up my head.

Emily Dickinson and Gerard Manley Hopkins

My notebook shows they took a formal cruise,
floated past bridges in the morning light.
From cliffs of fall to mid-Atlantic blues
they traveled fifteen knots the day her White
Election fell to his Ignatian news
of still pastures and feel-of-primrose night.
I owe my life to that New England nun
and triple locks the musing lover sprung.

In Amherst Emily prepared to risk it:
she scrawled some verse on napkins, tucked the wild
game in the hamper, doubled a batch of biscuit
dough, and stepped over her father's threshold
while the old man napped. Too timorous to ask it
— he may have dreamed her docile as a child —
Gerard approved, leaving his Company behind
for her improbable liquor, out of his mind.

The world they charged led soon to a famous wreck;
both saw it looming off the coast of Wales.
The demure velvet ribbon about her neck
was not a leash, and cautionary tales
rang true. Her cries rose with the waves on deck,
the lioness again, breasting the gales
that left her adamant to write the letter
granting each heart its stone for worse or better.

The first three drafts were bitter as dark beer.
The next seemed overlong; the fifth, too frantic.
She made a couplet timed to disappear

the instant one considered it pedantic
and for the stricken lute of the sonneteer
a veiled refrain of grief become romantic.
Not one would do. She'd have to write in bed.
He found her there and straightway lost his head.

She showed Gerard where he would find his own
pale eyes inside the velvet-tethered locket.
Poor Emily! How else could she have known
he carried Whitman in his greatcoat pocket?
It's best, I think, to leave the pair alone
until their dull dough sours on the captain's docket.
In any case there's no communion service
when this bread's gone and Emily is nervous.

How could she give him up to any storm
after the voyage shared — those breathless dashes —
a line all stress, or nearly so, a form
impervious as slag, set free of ashes.
Let others rest in harbor, safe and warm.
They found their comfort in the cold sea crashes
the black west sent to beat the soldier's cave;
that Roman collar carried to the grave,

laid like a wreath over the unmarked vault
where bones of ghostly lovers washed ashore
on her white beach. The sand ground from basalt
by wind and wave in the skull's unquiet roar
was soft-sift now, though powerless to halt
the glassed descent from ecstasy and more.
These brief affairs we label mid-Victorian,
seduce the timid soul of wit's historian.

"Gerard," Emily wrote, under a sky all sunset,
"It's over — like a tune — the sad Campaign
of Sting and Sweet — will never be the one let
soar — The Auctioneer of Parting — bid the rain
rehearse the dew." Her pen assailed the runlet
crossing the intimate sheet with a purple stain:
my Grandmother Dickinson, dyed in the clerical woof,
was warped for good. I am the living proof.

Greta Garbo and the Star Messenger

Her face the preface to water, stirred.
The least ripple widens out to the rim.
Minnows flicker up from the still bottom,
fins unwinding a silver discord.
Nothing is said. The arrested word
fades under indolent cloud. A faint drum
throbs in the temple's delirium
and disappears like the flight of a bird. ⸺

Alone in theatric dark, I feel her mood
inscribe the face I turn to the silver screen.
Secret lovers, rivers of solitude,
and a heaven of fixed stars maroon
the woman we know. On the island a reed
bends into the current and is gone.

Maria Callas, the Woman Behind the Legend

title from the biography
by Arianna Stassinopoulos

Her biographer gives us the woman, the artist:
two sides of a coin presenting
contrary faces. She calls the woman Maria,
the artist *La Callas*, a Greek
bearing gifts to Milan, darling and scourge of
La Scala and not to be trusted. When hecklers
tossed radishes onto the stage
La Callas smiled, ecstatic, gathered them to
her breast like the loveliest

                        roses. In her
fifties Maria asked, *Why doesn't anyone write*
an opera for Mary Magdalene? That
vision of washing a god's feet with her tears:
what convincing drama! I could have been
useful there: I carried my mother's genes for
histrionics, tear-ducts the most active
prop in my repertoire. Cried — not just from
remorse, depression, and worse. I cried
from relief, anger,

                    sudden noise, the exact
turn of a phrase, the terrors and joys
of total understanding. And drying the Savior's
feet with my hair: the image obsessed me,
though my skimpy locks had been
chopped off at three in hopes that short hair

would thicken. All over town, my sister's
luxuriant curls spilled from studio windows on
both sides of the block.

                      Maria, the man I've
found, man I will never marry,
calls me *La Maddalena.* My hair on the cutting-
room floor nearly white, it was
late luck invited him in. The art each of us
lives by, a country between us, keeps us
apart. Two faces of one coin at the going rate,
obverse joining reverse, close
to the other side.

George Eliot (Mary Ann Evans Cross)

She has... cultivated every art to make herself
attractive, feeling bitterly... what a struggle it
was, without beauty, whose influence she
exaggerates as do all ugly people.

LADY JEBB

Lost in her stories' complex flow, I drowned
the sorrows of adolescence, worked
through a reading list from my favorite
history teacher. The writer's life promised
more. Somewhere there had to exist
a man in love with a woman whose gift was the
mind alone. This is how I began
the solitary life, apart from domestic duties,
absent from mealtime chatter.

                    My idol preferred
subdued colors, hoping to fade into the
tasteful décor of the drawing room. Married or
not, no matter, her passionate
mind cut a swath through intellectual circles.
You would perhaps have been amused,
she writes, *to see an affectionate... dowdy*
friend splendid in grey moiré
antique — the consequence of a... lecture from
Owen Jones.

           If the long-banished nun sneaks into
my dressing-room mirror, into my
worst recurrent nightmare — the one with familiar

strangers proclaiming the common
life — I cross myself with Sister Margaret Jean
whose stroke or heart attack jangled the intricate
circuitry of her language. She
fought back, made her painful way to the fifth-
grade reader, checked out

                           with the switchboard
humming. Today I lift my receiver
to keep the important calls coming. Thanks to two
marginal women, I still have the word, the world
listening in.

FROM

Possible Sibyls

The Stirrups

Warts discovered me everywhere by natural right,
the ugly sister's curse, no matter how smart,
how clever, a blight on index finger,
sole of the foot, and more intimate parts,
the butt of comic effects I hated, even in Chaucer.
They appeared overnight, uninvited, they settled in,
they bled.

      The workhorse under my girlish weight
changed to a thoroughbred. Held by those broad
haunches and fantasy, I could
forget my warts, believe the night rode out to meet me.
What can I ask of night, if not
surcease from sorrow? Then, onto the scene, came
milkweed, the natural balm, and I was doomed
no longer.

      Every cure I had tried — cautery, knife,
foul-smelling Eskar Ointment, obscure
graves dug for knotted string: milkweed
replaced them all, the miracle-wing of prodigal seed
flung over alley and field.
What flowed in those wild veins, meeting my skin,
restored the clear morning. Heart so full, how

could I guess where the bridle paths led, how far
from the childhood field the horse
returned to a nag? Milkweed grew as before, a universal
weed, the cure no more than a lull
from stubborn warts in my head. Weekly now, my feet

in the stirrups, I lie in the sterile room,
tied to an old specific surrounded by Latin names.

Virus, they say, *and verruca, excrescences of the skin.*
Lie down, they say, and we'll treat you
with strong podophyllin. Far from the bitter resin,
the poison root, dense properties of mandrake
and mayapple, the passion-encumbered fruit. The sense
of the past cut off, this frayed rope in hand,
I grieve

        the live horse released from the dreaming
field to wander the fenced-in waste: the ghost
of something that mattered.

Crossarms

On a cold day, this six-foot stepladder's a hardship
post for washing the bay windows where a rude
bird — probably crow — let fly with droppings
that whitened and blocked the clear
prospect more than a year ago.

Newspapers recycled this morning, I polish the pane
to a fine gloss with rediscovered
poems — carefully chosen pages of *APR*. The whole sky
reflects in the window: thin wires
cut through the picture plane where a lone crow

watches from the telephone pole's crossarm. This
bird of twenty-three calls excels in the mimic
arts: whine of dog, squawk of hen, a voice almost
human. Why is he so silent?... Toodle-oo,
Good-bye, Yehuda Amichai, Translated by the Author.

And would you mind, I wonder, my buffing windows with
your lines? After your reading you would not
shake my hand. I felt rebuffed. *Religious reasons*
says a Jewish friend. Sometimes I do not
understand these tough exclusions.

Your poems make good things happen. The light comes
unobstructed. I couldn't tell you as you
scrawled your name with more I can't decipher on
the first blank page of *Great Tranquility*. I know
my next step is *Danger: Do Not Stand Here.* I

stand there. *You may lose your balance.* Now *that*
I can understand. Behind me, wind
sways the power lines. The crow holds steady. Ahead,
the poet's face looks out beside "The Water's Surface."
I toss the crumpled papers

at the ladder platform, shift my feet, miss, and see
that noble face go down. My neighbor
passes with a cheery warning. Time to grip the sash,
invoke Negative Capability, inform some other
body: Batman, the Flying Nun, the Wright Brothers.

       Tonight, below the danger line, I'll toss
newspapers into next week's recycle
bin. I check my work with pride. The window gives
everything back. The crow prepares for
flight, wears the committed look of graffiti artists.
Storm clouds move in. Soon the three of us
will sleep as one, our names written on water.

In the middle of Priest Lake

            Sister Margaret Clare
ships the oars and takes off her veil,
her coif. Not long ago I was her high-school student.
Her starched bandeau comes off, wind
riffles her hair. She runs her fingers through
a modified crew cut while I hesitate, eyes
half-closed, unwilling

                    to stare or look away.
"Take yours off," she says. "It feels great!" and
before I know it, I've unpinned the veil, loosened
the coif strings, lifted the white band
for a sail. I salute the black-and-white headdress
blown from the mast
of my upraised arm, the freedom

                    I love unfurled
without warning. I'm a lifer committed to sunshine,
to ambient air
as suddenly knowing incurable need
I savor the small pleasure
given up — now given back — in the middle of this lake
miles from the difficult shore
Mother Superior holds fast.

Blueprints

From a long way off I can see the cross-
hatching. This anonymous man of the Plain
People of Lancaster County laid out

more than 100 barns, not depending on blue-
prints. *It's just a talent the Lord gave me.*
I can close my eyes and see the whole

structure sitting there. Sitting there,
alert for the whole structure, I count
thirty-three question-mark forms under wide-brimmed hats

bent to a common task against the Prussian blue
blank of sky. My fingers trace a slow X
of suspenders, the unknown articles of risk

and faith in a landscape of minor mercies. *This*
one touched my heart, says the planner, asking
that his name be forgotten. The barn

belonged to a burned-out widow. People came from
miles around. The barn was raised again, clean
grain of the wood stood vertical, all knots

wrestled into a pattern. Translating this morning
the visual text into words, I ask that my name be remembered,
that the legend over my grave

be the planner's. *This one touched my heart.*

Living by the Water

The reservoir we drank from fills
and fills again, unending
as the coastal rain that swells it.
The water-table rises, old roads washed out
and small craft swept to sea.
Until the storm front passes, let me stay
clear of your tilted deck: no other way to be
left out of the one place I cannot
walk on water.

         When we slept, dry-eyed
on the shores of Babylon, how did we
hang our harp on the willow branch in this
strange land? Pale reed
beside the water, my water-sign
a wand depending on the hidden spring.
I see how water carves the wale
of the corduroy cliff and throws
great boulders on its wheel

              to round
these urns for burial. How water lifts
columns of basalt, cutting its own
bright path, jagged down the mountain.
My fingers graze the smooth amphoras in these
tidepools, Greek to me. I feel the darkness
coming on. Like the sea,
I gather wool and the wool I gather is another
kind of crying to that gull

                        sailing the lower
air and dying slowly back into the wave.
I blame these phases on the moon but can't deny
the tides we've known. A circle in her beak
brings water, sharp horns
mean wind. This is the place we started out,
the place we've always been. And now good-bye,
the path forks here. I am my own
barometer, and like the water, always falling.

Beside Mill River

When my key sticks in the neighbor's
lock and I finally click, it's the wrong
keyhole, the wrong garage; when my feet,
on automatic pilot,
pause at the common door like the Levittown
ghost who forgets to count, anonymous tenant in a Queens
row house, I conjure up
the unique interior.

When the six o'clock news
overflows every lintel, and the identical chicken
stews in dozens of seasoned pots;
when the Sunday beef
simmers through a slow, canned sermon
I trundle my laundry to the ten-cent center
or turn again to the run of the river
that is not at all, or almost
never the same.

Except that the river
repeats the memorable
falls over and over — the same cold invitation of moss
and ice. Across the bridge
light flickers darkly
through curtained glass, and I feel the foreshortened
breath drawing me over the edge: the imagined
embrace in the drowned
high-rise of sleep.

Dialogue Partly Platonic

When we met by chance at the letter
drop on a cold bright
day in early spring, I was in jeans
and a blue beret. I remember your
jacket — suede — when we
walked, surprised by
ourselves on the sudden street, into
each other's arms. Denim and
suede and the time to stop.

In a house more ancient than brick
and beam, where the chant of
cloisters rose and fell
and the stern-browed portraits
looked askance, we circled the crypt
by candle gleam in the intricate
steps of a formal dance, threading
the mazes carefully,
measuring every syllable.

When the record ends and letters fade
when the tape runs out on the poem's
reel where the shadows lie
in the candle glow and the house
embodies its women still, here is
the cave I would have you
know. Reenter it now, mounting
the steps to your troubled sleep
in the upstairs dark.

In the locker room

        I surprise the women
dressed in their bodies: in breasts,
knees, eyebrows, pubic
hair. Excitable children appear
to accept them. Pitted and fat, dazzling
and golden, the women
drowse under the shower, a preview of
bodies the children try on
with their eyes.

        At sixty-five, I am less than
a child, whose mother walked
fearfully clothed, afraid of the water.
My grip on the towel gives me away. I move
into the pool suitably over my head
past my mother's responsible
daughter. Later, wild to learn, I practice
standing alone — only my underpants on —
under the gun
of the hair dryer.

        A queen-size woman
sweetly accosts me, recommends
more clothes. Someone has pointed out
a peekaboo crack in the men's
locker room. "What a shame," she intones,
"such a nice clean
club." I loiter in my underwear
worn out with surveillance.
What we don't know
won't hurt us.

Oh, but it does deprive us!
These ravenous mermaids
stripped to their scales, swim from
the framed reproductions, pale and diaphanous
planes engineered for unmistakable
languor. Something has changed
in the changing room where we step out of
lingerie meant for the fainting couch
and bring on the body in person.

Spiritual Exercises

Knees up! Sophie shouts. We're jogging in place,
one mild gigolo and a pool full of women —
teens to seniors — with every physique
in the book. Madison Avenue gods call our drill-
sergeant a Full Figure. I call her
No Jiggles, read *solid state.* Strong as a
tugboat with plenty of
cargo in tow, she's pulling us through
holy routines: Little-Engines- clenching weak
ankles That-Could tie themselves in
French knots.

> *Flat on the bottom!* Sophia yells at
our feet, her short blond cut
unruffled as the blue cool of ecstatic eyes.
Is it *my* bottom or the pool's? I can't
see through the roily water past the hard rock
drowning out measured
instruction. Just when I'm sneaking a look at the
hour, she tells us to do
Pendulums. Elbows flexed, lifted high, my lower arms
sweep inward and out: Grandmother Clock in
brassy precision.

> Tanned statuesque, the Amazon
goddess floats her breasts on water
I try not to swallow. Birds flutter from nests of
Mother Wren's arthritic fingers. When music turns
mellow I know that we're cooling down to
the moment for gliding: *left, swoop, pointed toes,*

wrists leading the body to
paradise-under-the-shower. *Olé!* I say, meaning
Oil-of-, fighting the locker-room bull,
lathering supple attachments. A long stretch for the
beach towel, heavenly clothes.

What I mistook for heather

was creeping thyme the gardener said,
and I watched it creeping
over the sheer rockfall without a leg
to stand on. "So delicate," a neighbor
said, preferring thyme to sturdier
plants, the day she made that confident
pronouncement. Just out of sight
the raspberry canes waited for something
to lean on. When I planted my foot
in the flower bed, it felt like the first
far step across the moon.

Shadegrown Tobacco

for Richard Hugo (1923–1982)

Tobacco wraiths are back. Their pale arms
flutter in the grassy field
and you are in your 14th dream, the letters
white confetti round your bed. I want to say:
Cured, the wide green leaves of this New England
shed, old rituals call us to the place
we started out, the edge.

                    I'm walking in a gale.
The metal STOP signs flap like paper
by the cold motel where I step into the traffic.
The flag reads: HEMLOCK   DEAD END STREET
All the great men of our past — Washington, Monroe,
Jefferson, Taft — cross and recross the thoroughfare
on their way to the wild
Pacific where you are. I'm coming too.

                   The gulls
own Haystack Rock; this coast belongs to me. You own
a run of jacks, their gray mouths
own the sea. No thread-and-scissors men,
these three in oilskins who tend
and spin the giant vacuum, suck dirty air or water
from the storm drains.

                The severed line may not be
vital but a fatal twist cuts off
the span their laws determine. Not Zeus himself

can override the Fates, nor madness rescue.
Opponents rise like dragon's teeth in furrows. More
myths you would have said
you didn't know, pretending
not to read.

        Ecola Park, tobacco wraiths move west
where great ferns cluster
on the woodland path. I watch them
laying down their swords
and in the aftermath, dark berries of salal.
No one owns the wind you love. The phantom lung
demands its fill of air. Shrill kites
own the clouds and sheer
sun falls into ocean.

        You would have loved these three
hard-drinking men, nothing phony about them:
a crew you'd like to spend time with
in a bar. And now you've crossed it in your fancy
salmon boat. Or better yet, waded out into the stream
leaving us with the big dreamfish
you and Yeats were after.

        Wherever I am, Dick, I want you
to know I'll keep you close as a coat in gray weather,
your voice strong in my ear, falling
like these coastal rains
to fill the reservoir or float the Big Sky home,
riding your favorite thermals. The clouds
not gauze or birds of prey, but raw
silk umbrellas gliding the wind, the shroud lines
tough and holding with your abandoned towns.

In the Whirlpool

Focused on the middle distance, my eyes avoid
her airspace. My toes collide
with another human
foot. Quickly, I withdraw the look
lost between clock and infinity. "Sorry,
I wasn't paying... Do you
swim every day?" Her name is Eva Perl.
Her accent is German. Now that we're warming up
I brag — modestly — "I started at nine
laps and have just leveled off
at thirteen."

        Her gaze is straight on. "I have
no ambitions," she says,
the sheen of her hair floating
silver in steam. It is not a rebuke. She may
be a sibyl. "I'm seventy-eight and lucky
to swim at all." Silence returns
the machine we are part of, caught in this
distance, the bubble and fall,
an ocean between us. I want to bridge it.
To follow this Eva

          preparing to leave. "I hope
I'm like you when I'm seventy-eight."
She looks back without smiling. "It's been
by ups and downs," she remarks, climbing up.
I think of the photographs — the heaped
anonymous fingers and feet. Of what is required
to move past intrusion. The mother-of-pearl

luminous coat, shell that encloses,
the wall I must build
to come to terms with this alien body.

The Widows of Mykonos

Seeing their black weeds in terrible sun, the other
life that holds their gaze
unswerving in the village street, I recognize
the miles I've come to find this land
Henry Miller calls *all stone*
and light.

My steps are sagging stone, meandering
through the patterned square, my heart
not light but shrouded, a house closed up, its flutter
caught in that familiar net
of shuttered grief.

The skyborne song turns hollow
in a maze of stone, the light a torture
and the dark a cave. I carve the epitaph in some
illusionary code
the scholars cannot break and bury what remains
under toppled stone.

Legend in stone relief, light
breaks in half across the blue Aegean,
night floods the whitening shore. Along stone walls
the full-face light, without slant or shadow,
falls, leaving no stone unturned.

Hagios Panaghiotes: The Church in Tolon

Feeling nervous, out of place and halfway through
the Greek Orthodox Sunday service, I realize
from certain headlong illuminations
I'm on the wrong side — the men's — but not enough
to do anything
important. At the votive stand, a widow
blows out candles, lights a few, the order
random as the genuflections of the priest, and I
am in a foreign land.

      Ensconced in a separate
altitude, the cleric gives us
his back, small acolyte on the line, bobbing
when the leader
bobs. Through his beard, the priest intones
familiar versicles. As in a Brueghel
painting, what matters
happens on the edge. The cantors
cant. The women move their lips in silent
intercession. The shady incense drifts
above our heads.

     Demented chandeliers: crystal
and gold in clouds of plastic. The bearded
saints look down — martyr and mystic — bald, severely
drawn. All of us are old. The operation
was successful, but the patient
stars flicker to a halo in the dome. Long ago,
schooled to fight distraction

to levitate — that is, *make light,* as in Marvell's
Center of Knowledge — I learned to wait
on the dead. Light the candle one more time.

The Garden of Botanical Delights

1

At the Public Market, salmon in hand, we
examine the *Brassica*,
children of the wild cabbage laid out with
botanical fervor: collards, turnip,
mustard and kale, broccoli, brussels sprouts
and the queen of them all,
kohlrabi.

When I was the bride of Sorrow
and carried his poison
tips in my quiver, the arrows pointed toward
my own unsinkable heart, pain
the proof I needed on the brink of my being
alive with the pulse of
disaster.

Today in a transparent season,
stalking the stalk plant, I hear the stream in my veins
run faster. I no longer wish to count
myself a Cabbage Planter — my figure for those
who feel nothing — the too-stolid head
balanced above steady ground.

2

Here is my act of faith in the secret life of
plants, the still more secret
lives we harbor in our sleep when images
float upward into light

and everything that grows
begins to speak: *Tension along the midriff,*

consternation among the broccoli. The several
heads rising from a single
stalk, the many voices of bok choy. We wade
all night into the darkening
window, the living room slowly filled by
the river, cover our bodies

with silt from deepening beds like women who
darken their eyelids with kohl.
The life we hold in common with the common
vegetable tells us to furnish our house
with sun, with air and rain: whatever
the current carries.

3

What is the root of this passion for
classified information, sensors
fine-tuned as hairs on the pods of white
mustard? One scientist
devised a scheme for breaking the genus
in five, alive as the odd-numbered
senses, a plan based on leaf-buds,
on flowers.

For hours this morning, I
pored over the Lindley charts, a kindly
student of taxonomy. Dearest,
late as it is in love's perennial
summer, all my terminal buds
are active and open, flowers abortive

and succulent, ready
for harvest.

My vanished lover,
come back to volatile oils
distilled from seeds of black mustard,
to the leaf mustard's
gathered rosette. This cool-season
variety shoots to seed
later than the usual white. Salads
postponed;

you are sorely missed in your
good garden. Like the steady green of a
cover crop, yours was a notable leaving.

4

When the plant dies back into the seed
the missing language flowers. Linked
words stretch their chains across

the continent, the ink and circuitry
of winter culture. Your crisp Italian
consonants roll across my tongue:

brocco, brocco, the shoot that turns
diminutive as broccoli. This singular
crop exists chiefly in the plural,

its Latinate form one of many seeds
from which this poem grows. Hold on to
the root and note the piccolo's

slant rhyme in *broccolo,* the salmon's
uphill climb into receding rivers,
and the other name for the wild

ancestor: sea cabbage. Into that tide
I plunge again and again
until the next spring floodtime.

      5

If I were one of the herd
turned out by my lord
to pasture, I'd dream of
the drumhead cabbage,
the thousand-headed kale.

Browsing the grassy knoll
I'd find my vegetative
life enough. This
intermittent lack beyond
the livestock in our lives

where far-off summits lift
and fall, might disappear
as scant light slowly
changed the scale
of what we shall not want.

Then take these flowers,
too long borne like a cross,
and hang them where
the brick walls ring
exultant in a dying chant:

I cannot love my yield
the less because of this
late gathering.

Acknowledgments

These poems have been taken from: *From the Darkroom*, Bobbs-Merrill (1964); *When Sky Lets Go*, George Braziller (1978); *Magpie on the Gallows*, Copper Canyon Press (1982); *The Light Station on Tillamook Rock*, Arrowood Books (1990); *Imaginary Ancestors*, Broken Moon Press (1991); *Possible Sibyls*, Lynx House Press (1991); and *Double Dutch*, a chapbook, Red Wing Press (1999).

Imaginary Ancestors first appeared as a chapbook from *CutBank*/SmokeRoot Press (1978).

The Light Station on Tillamook Rock first appeared as a Collectors Limited Edition from The Press of Appletree Alley (in 1989).

Thanks to editors of the following publications in which these poems originally appeared, some in slightly different form:

Calapooya Collage: "Going Back to the Convent," "Still Life," and "Woman Locked in a Memorial Museum"

Clackamas Literary Review: "On Western Avenue behind a Horse-and-Buggy," "Widows Riding Amtrak"

Crazyhorse: "Sapphires in the Mud"

The Paris Review: "Surgery Waiting," "Balancing Acts," and "Metempsychosis"

River City: "Double Dutch"

The San Diego Reader: "To Marilyn Monroe Whose Favorite Color Was White"

Seattle Poets & Photographers: A Millennium Reflection, edited by J.T. Stewart and Rod Slemmons, Seattle Arts Commission, University of Washington Press: "Peregrine Falcons in the Bank Tower"

The Southern California Anthology: "Vermeer's *A Woman Holding a Balance*"

The Yale Review: "Almanac"

"Still Life" and "Woman Locked in a Memorial Museum" are two of three poems that won the Carolyn Kizer Award.

"Vermeer's *A Woman Holding a Balance*" won the Ann Stanford Prize.

The following poems also appeared in *Double Dutch*, Red Wing Press (1999): "Still Life," "Double Dutch," and "Vermeer's *A Woman Holding a Balance*."

I also wish to express my thanks to the poet-editors of some of these books: Richard Howard, Sam Hamill, Lex Runciman, Christopher Howell, and Quinton Duval.

Thanks, too, to John Ellison and Lesley Link of Broken Moon Press and to the friends whose suggestions have been helpful: Thomas Aslin, Abe Opin-car, Patricia Solon, Joan Swift, and Gary Thompson. Finally, I am deeply grateful to Barbara Evans, who put her own life on hold to make time for editing and computerizing my typescript.

About the Author

Madeline DeFrees was educated at St. Mary's Academy, Portland, Oregon, and went on to earn the B.A. from Marylhurst College, in Lake Oswego, Oregon, and the M.A. from the University of Oregon. She studied poetry for brief periods with Karl Shapiro, Robert Fitzgerald, and John Berryman.

DeFrees has received fellowships in poetry from the John Simon Guggenheim Foundation and the National Endowment for the Arts. She has also published essays, reviews, and seventeen short stories.

Teaching assignments include seventeen years at Holy Names College (renamed Fort Wright College), Spokane; twelve at the University of Montana, Missoula; and six at the University of Massachusetts, Amherst. Since her retirement in 1985, she has held residencies at Bucknell University, Eastern Washington University, and Wichita State University.

The Chinese character for poetry is made up of two parts: "word" and "temple." It also serves as pressmark for Copper Canyon Press.

Founded in 1972, Copper Canyon Press remains dedicated to publishing poetry exclusively, from Nobel laureates to new and emerging authors. The Press thrives with the generous patronage of readers, writers, booksellers, librarians, teachers, students, and funders — everyone who shares the conviction that poetry invigorates the language and sharpens our appreciation of the world.

PUBLISHERS' CIRCLE

Allen Foundation for the Arts
Lannan Foundation
Lila Wallace–Reader's Digest Fund
National Endowment for the Arts

EDITORS' CIRCLE

Breneman Jaech Foundation
Port Townsend Paper Company
Washington State Arts Commission

For information and catalogs:

COPPER CANYON PRESS
Post Office Box 271
Port Townsend, Washington 98368
360/385-4925
poetry@coppercanyonpress.org
www.coppercanyonpress.org

The font used here is Font Bureau Californian, originally designed by
Frederic Goudy in 1938 for the University of California Press.
Carol Twombly and David Berlow contributed to this digitized version.
Book design by Valerie Brewster, Scribe Typography.
Printed on archival-quality Glatfelter Author's Text
by McNaughton & Gunn, Inc.